Top 10 Secrets That Every Business Owner Must Know To Double Leads, Sales and Profits In The Next 90 Days!

by Robert Tucker

COPYRIGHT AND DISCLAIMER

Published by:
Leader Publishing Worldwide
19 Axford Bay
Port Moody, BC V3H 3R4
Tel: 1 888 294 9151
Fax: 1 877 575 9151
Website: www.noresults-nofee.com

PRINTED IN 2019

DEDICATION

I would like to dedicate this book to so many people. Thank you to my Mother who showed me how to become independent and always take a chance in life. To my Dad who showed me what loyalty and dedication means. To Janie (my Jane Jane), who has shown me what it means to be truly happy and live and love each day. To my Daughter, Mary, who is the epitome of focus, determination and keeping the goal in sight. To my Son, Reece, who is the example you see in Websters when you look up loving, caring and happy.

I wouldn't be here today without all of you!

Robert Tucker

CONTENTS

INTRODUCTION

Congratulations in your quest to enhance your business and marketing skills. This is only the first step to achieving your goals and dreams but it will set the foundation for growth and success!

As I began to research this book, I thought back to the beginning of my business career. I was freshly out of the military and started a company that failed miserably! I went from thinking that I had it made (about to be bought out for millions) to liquidated, homeless and less than $100 in my pocket in the span of 7 days. That caused me to seek out knowledge that I didn't have and approach the next business from a completely different perspective. That was after a few days of sulking of course.

In choosing my next business I made sure to find mentors and coaches from whom I could learn. I learned there are 3 lines to the adage "a wise man learns from his mistakes." What most don't hear is "a wiser man learns from other people's mistakes," but "the wisest man learns from other people's success!" That was about the time that I started my next business and was named International Rookie of the Year. I went on to develop franchises and start and sell other businesses using the same proven principles, methods and techniques. I made sure to find coaches and mentors to teach me and hold me accountable to my goals.

As you read the principles to follow, remember it does not matter what industry nor type of business you operate. What matters is that you grasp the heart of the principles, the underlying lessons and strategies, that can help grow any operation in any category of business imaginable.

Start NOW, not tomorrow, not next week or next year.

Yours in success,
Robert Tucker

PS. If you would like to arrange a meeting to get a profitable third party perspective on your business, please send an email to Robert@RobertTucker.com and we will gladly point you in the right direction.

To learn how to avoid the 3 key mistakes all small business owners make, visit www.RobertTuckerUniversity.com

1

Creating a Powerful Offer

I'm not going to beat around the bush on this one:

Your offer is the granite foundation of your marketing campaign.

Get it right, and everything else will fall into place. Your headline will grab readers, your copy will sing, your ad layout will hardly matter, and you will have customers running to your door.

Get it wrong, and even the best looking, best-written campaign will sink like the Titanic.

A powerful offer is an irresistible offer. It's an offer that gets your audience frothing at the mouth and clamoring over each other all the way to your door. An offer that makes your readers pick up the phone and open their wallets.

Irresistible offers make your potential customers think, "I'd be crazy not to take him up on that," or "An offer like this doesn't come around very often." They instill a sense of emotion, of desire, and ultimately, urgency.

Make it easy for customers to purchase from you the first time, and spend your time keeping them coming back.

I'll say it again: **get it right, and everything else will fall into place.**

The Crux of Your Marketing Campaign

As you work your way through this program, you will find that nearly every chapter discusses the importance of a powerful offer as related to your marketing strategy or promotional campaign.

There's a reason for this. The powerful offer is more often than not the reason a customer will open their wallets. It is how you generate leads, and then convert them into loyal customers. The more dramatic, unbelievable, and valuable the offer is the more dramatic and unbelievable the response will be.

Many companies spend thousands of dollars on impressive marketing campaigns in glossy magazines and big city newspapers. They send massive direct mail campaigns on a regular basis; yet don't receive an impressive or massive response rate.

These companies do not yet understand that simply providing information on their company and the benefits of their product is not enough to get customers to act. There is no reason to pick up the phone or visit the store, *right now.*

Your powerful, irresistible offer can:

- Increase leads
- Drive traffic to your website or business
- Move old product
- Convert leads into customers
- Build your customer database

What Makes a Powerful Offer?

A powerful offer is one that makes the most people respond, and take action. It gets people running to spend money on your product or service.

Powerful offers nearly always have an element of *urgency* and of *scarcity*. They give your audience a reason to act immediately, instead of put it off until a later date.

Urgency relates to time. The offer is only available until a certain date, during a certain period of the day, or if you act within a few hours of seeing the ad. The customer needs to act now to take advantage of the offer.

Scarcity related to quantity. There are only a certain number of customers who will be able to take advantage of the offer. There may be a limited number of spaces, a limited number of products, or simply a limited number of people the business will provide the offer to. Again, this requires that customer acts immediately to reap the high value for low cost.

Powerful offers also:

Offer great value. Customers perceive the offer as having great value – more than a single product on its own, or the product at its regular price. It is clear that the offer takes the reader's needs and wants into consideration.

Make sense to the reader. They are simple and easy to understand if read quickly. Avoid percentages – use half off or 2 for 1 instead of 50% off. There are no "catches" or requirements; no fine print.

Seem logical. The offer doesn't come out of thin air. There is a logical reason behind it – a holiday, end of season, anniversary celebration, or new product. People can get suspicious of offers that seem "too good to be true" and have no apparent purpose.

Provide a premium. The offer provides something extra to the customer, like a free gift, or free product or service. They feel they are getting something extra for no extra cost. Premiums are perceived to have more value than discounts.

Remember that when your target market reads your offer, they will be asking the following questions:

1. What are you offering me?
2. What's in it for me?
3. What makes me sure I can believe you?
4. How much do I have to pay for it?

The Most Powerful Types of Offers

Decide what kind of offer will most effectively achieve your objectives. Are you trying to generate leads, convert customers, build a database, move old product off the shelves, or increase sales?

Consider what type of offer will be of most value to your ideal customers – what offer will make them act quickly.

Free Offer

This type of offer asks customers to act immediately in exchange for something free. This is a good strategy to use to build a customer database or mailing list. Offer a free consultation, free consumer report, or other item of low cost to you but of high perceived value.

You can also advertise the value of the item you are offering for free. For example, act now and you'll receive a free consultation, worth $75 dollars. This will dramatically increase your lead generation, and allow you to focus on conversion when the customer comes through the door or picks up the phone.

The Value Added Offer

Add additional services or products that cost you very little, and combine them with other items to increase their attractiveness. This increases the perception of value in the customer's mind, which will justify increasing the price of a product or service without incurring extra hard costs to your business.

Package Offer

Package your products or services together in a logical way to increase the perceived value as a whole. Discount the value of the package by a small margin, and position it as a "start-up kit" or "special package." By packaging goods of mixed values, you will be able to close more high-value sales. For example: including a free desk-jet printer with every computer purchase.

Premium Offer

Offer a bonus product or service with the purchase of another. This strategy will serve your bottom line much better than discounting. This includes 2 for 1 offers, offers that include free gifts, and in-store credit with purchases over a specific dollar amount.

Urgency Offer

As I mentioned above, offers that include an element of urgency enjoy a better response rate, as there is a reason for your customers to act immediately. Give the offer a deadline or limit the number of spots available.

Guarantee Offer

Offer to take the risk of making a purchase away from your customers. Guarantee the performance or results of your product or service, and offer to compensate the customer with their money back if they are not satisfied. This will help overcome any fear or reservations about your product, and make it more likely for your leads to become customers.

Create Your Powerful Offer

1. Pick a single product or service.

Focus on only one product or service – or one product or service *type* – at a time. This will keep your offer clear, simple, and easy to understand. This can be an area of your business you wish to grow, or old product that you need to move off the shelves.

2. Decide what you want your customers to do.

What are you looking to achieve from your offer? If it is to generate more leads, then you'll need your customer to contact you. If it is to quickly sell old product, you'll need your customer to come into the store and buy it. Do you want them to visit your website? Sign up for your newsletter? How long do they have to act? Be clear about your call to action, and state it clearly in your offer.

3. Dream up the biggest, best offer.

First, think of the biggest, best things you could offer your customers – regardless of cost and ability. Don't limit yourself to a single type of offer, combine several types of offers to increase value. Offer a premium, plus a guarantee, with a package offer. Then take a look at what you've created, and make the necessary changes so it is realistic.

4. Run the numbers.

Finally, make sure the offer will leave you with some profit – or at least allow you to break even. You don't want to publish an outrageous offer that will generate a tremendous number of leads, but leave you broke. Remember that each customer has an acquisition cost, as well as a lifetime value. The amount of their first purchase may allow you to break even, but the amount of their subsequent purchases may make you a lovely profit.

2

Use Scripts to Increase Sales Immediately

What do playbooks, prompts, guides and scripts all have in common?

They are all popular tools that dictate or guide human behavior toward a desired outcome.

Playbooks help coaches tell sports teams specifically how to play the game to overcome an opponent. Prompts help to kick-start writers and other creative professionals when stuck in a rut. Guides provide a series of instructions so that a person or team of people can complete or implement a specific task. Film scripts tell actors how to act for a particular part.

If you're in the business of sales, you also know about sales scripts. Sales scripts are tools that guide salespeople during interactions or conversations with potential customers.

A large number of businesses use scripts, either as a way of maintaining consistency amongst a sales team, training new salespeople, or enhancing their sales skills. They may have a single script, or several, and may change their scripts regularly, or use the same one for years.

13

What most businesses overlook, however, is that the sales script is a living, breathing, changing member of their sales team. They may be internal documents, but they deserve just as much time and effort as your marketing collateral.

Do You Really Need a Script?

The short answer is yes. You absolutely need a script for any and every customer interaction you and your salespeople may find yourselves in.

Sure, countless business owners and salespeople work every day without a script. If you own your own business, chances are you're already a pretty good salesperson. But if you are not using scripts, you're only working at half of your true potential – or half of your potential earnings.

Scripts don't have to be "cheesy" or read verbatim. They act as a map for your sales process, and provide prompts to trigger your memory and keep you on track. How many times have you made a cold call that didn't work out the way you wanted it to? Scripts dramatically improve the effectiveness and efficiency of your sales processes.

A comprehensive set of scripts will also keep a level of consistency amongst your salespeople and the customer service they provide your clients.

Once scripts are written, memorized, and rehearsed, they become like film scripts; the salesperson can breathe their own life and personality into the conversation, while staying focused on the call's objectives.

Why Your Scripts Aren't Working

If you a currently using scripts in your business, are they working? Are they as effective as they could possibly be? How do you know? When was the last time they were reviewed or updated?

Scripts are like any other element of your marketing campaign – they need to be tested and measured for results, and changed based on what is or is not working.

Measure the success of your script based on your conversion rates. Of all the people you speak to and use the script, how many are being converted from leads to sales?

When evaluating your existing scripts, ask yourself the following questions:

How old is this script? What was it written for? Scripts are living, breathing members of your company. They need to be written and rewritten and rewritten again as the needs of your customers change, your product or services change, or as new strategies are implemented.

Does this script address all the customer objections we regularly hear? Every time you hear a customer raise an objection that is not included on the script, add it. The power of your script lies in the ability to anticipate customer concerns, and answer them before they're raised.

Does this script sound the same as the others? Your scripts are part of the package that represents you as a company. There should be a consistent feel or approach throughout your scripts that your customers will recognize and feel confident dealing with.

Is everyone using the script? Who on your team regularly uses these scripts? Just the junior staff? Only the top-performing staff? Make sure everyone is singing from the same song sheet – your customers will appreciate the consistency.

Types of Scripts

Depending on the product or service you offer and the marketing strategies you have chosen, there are countless types of scripts you could potentially prepare for your business,

When you sit down to create your scripts, it would be wise to start by making a list of all the instances you and your staff members interact with your existing or potential customers. Then, prioritize the list from most to least important, and start writing from the top.

Here are some commonly used scripts, and their purposes:

Sales presentation script

Each time you or your sales staff make a presentation, they should be using the same or a slightly modified version of the same script. This script will include sample icebreakers, a presentation on benefits and features of the product or service, and a list of possible objections and responses. These scripts should also help alleviate some of the nervousness or anxiety associated with public speaking.

Closing script

Closing scripts help you do just that: close the sale. This could include a list of closing prompts or statements to get the transaction started. This type of script also includes a list of possible customer objections, and planned responses.

Incoming phone call script

Everyone who calls your business should be treated the same way; consistent information should be gathered and provided to the customer. The person answering the phone should state the company name, department name, and their own name in the initial greeting. This goes for both the main line, and each individual or department extension.

Cold call script

This is one of the most important scripts you can perfect for your business. The cold call script must master the art of quickly getting the attention of the customer, then engaging and persuading them with the benefits of the product or service. The caller needs to establish common ground with the potential customer, and find a way to get them talking through open-ended questions.

Direct mail follow-up script

Scripts for outgoing calls that are intended to follow up on a direct mail piece are essential for every direct mail campaign. They are designed to call qualified leads that have already received information and an offer, and convert them into customers. These scripts should focus on enticing customers to act, and overcoming any objections that may have prevented them from acting sooner.

Market research script

Scripts that are used primarily for the purpose of gathering information should be designed to get the customer talking. A focus on open-ended questions and relationship building statements will help to relax the customer, and encourage honest dialogue.

Difficult customer script

Just like every salesperson needs to practice the sales process, you and your staff also need to practice your ability to handle difficult customers. If you operate a retail business this is especially important, as difficult customers often present themselves in front of other customers. These scripts should help you diffuse the situation, calm the customer down, and then handle their objections.

Creating Scripts

Creating powerful scripts is not a complicated exercise, but it will take some time to complete. Focus on the most vital scripts for your business first, and engage the assistance of your sales staff in drafting or reviewing the scripts.

Your Script Binder

Keep master copies of all of your scripts in one organized place. An effective way to do this is to create a binder, and use tabs to separate each type of script.

You will also want to create a separate tab for customer objections, and list every single customer objection you have ever heard in relation to your product or service. Find a way to organize each objection so you can easily find them – group them by category or separate them with tabs.

Then, list your responses next to each objection – there should be several responses to each objection created with different customer types in mind. A master list of customer objections and responses is an invaluable tool for any business owner, salesperson, and script writer. The more responses you can think of, the better.

Remember, the script binder is never "finished." You will need to make sure that it is updated and added to on a regular basis.

Writing Scripts — Step by Step

Step One: Record What You're Doing Now

If you aren't using scripts – or even if you are – start by recording yourself in action. Use video or audio recording to tape yourself on the phone, in a sales presentation, or with a customer.

Make notes on your body language, word choice, customer reaction and body language, responses to objections, and closing statements.

You may also wish to ask an associate to make notes on your performance and discuss them with you in a constructive fashion.

Step Two: Evaluate What You're Doing Wrong

Take a look at your notes, and ask yourself the following questions:

- How are you engaging the customer?
- Are you building common ground and trust?
- Does what you are saying matter to the customer?
- Is your offer a powerful one?
- What objections are raised?
- How are you dealing with them?
- What objections are you avoiding?
- How natural is your close?
- Are you as effective as you think you can be?

Once you have answered and made notes in response to these questions, make a list of things you need to improve, and how you think you might go about doing so. Do you need to strengthen your closing statements? Do you need to brainstorm more responses to objections? Remember that everyone's script and sales process can be improved.

Step Three: Decide Who the Script is For

So now that you know the elements of your script you need to work on, you can begin drafting your new script, or revising an old one.

The first part of writing a script – or any piece of marketing material – is having a strong understanding of who you are writing it for. Who is your target audience? What does your ideal customer look like? Consider demographic characteristics like age, sex, location, income, occupation and marital status. Be as specific as possible. What are their purchase patterns? What motivates them to spend money?

If you are writing a cold call script, you will need to develop or purchase a list of people who fall into the target market specifics you have established. If you are writing a sales script for in-store customers, then spend some time reviewing what types of customers find their way into your place of business.

You will want to use words that your target audience will not only understand, but relate to and resonate with. Use sensory language that will trigger emotional and feeling responses – *I need this, this will solve that problem, I'll feel better if I have this, etc.*

Step Four: Decide What You Want to Say

There are typically five sections of every script – and there may be more, depending on the type and purpose of script:

1. Engage

- Get their attention or pique their interest
- Establish common ground
- Build trust, be human
- Ask for their time

2. Ask + Qualify

- Take control of the conversation by asking questions
- Focus on open-ended questions that cannot be answered with a "yes" or "no"
- Get the customer talking
- Ask as many questions as you need to get information on the customer's needs and purchase motivations

3. Get Agreement

- Ask closed-ended questions you are sure they will respond with "yes"
- Get them to agree on the benefits of the product or service
- Repeat key points back to the customer to gain agreement

4. Overcome Objections

- Anticipate objections based on customer comments, then refute them
- Make informative assumptions about their thought process, identify with their concern, then refute it using your own experiences
- Repeat concerns back to the customer to let them know you have heard them
- Ask about any remaining objections before you close

5. Close

- Assume that you have overcome all objections, and have the sale
- Ask the customer transactional questions, like delivery timing and payment method
- Be as confident and natural as possible

Step Five: Train Your Staff

Once you have written your company's scripts, you will need to ensure your staff understand and are comfortable using them.

Consider having a team meeting, and use role play to review each of the scripts. This will encourage your salespeople to practice amongst each other, and strengthen their sales skills. Ask them for feedback on the scripts, and make any necessary changes.

You will also need to decide how comfortable you are having your salespeople personalizing the scripts to suit their own styles. Be clear what elements of the script are "company standards" and essential techniques, but also be flexible with your team.

Step Six: Continually Revise

After you have carefully crafted your script, put it to the test. Practice on your colleagues, friends, and family. Get their feedback, and make changes.

Remember that scripts will need to change and evolve as your business changes and evolves, and new products or services are introduced. Keep your script binder on your desk at all times, and continually make changes and improvements to it.

You may also wish to record and evaluate your performance on a regular basis. This is an exercise you could incorporate into regular employee reviews, to use as a constructive tool for staff development.

Script Tips

- Practice anticipating and eliciting real objections – including the ones your customer doesn't want to raise.

- Make the script yours – it should look, feel, and sound like you naturally do, not like you're reading off the page.

- Spend time with the masters. If there is a salesperson you admire in your community, ask to observe them in action. Take notes on their performance, and the techniques they use for success.

- If your script is not successful, ask the customer why not? Even if you don't get the sale, you'll get a new objection you can craft responses to and never get stumped by it again.

- Don't fear objections. Just spend time identifying as many as possible, then practice overcoming them.

- Never stop thinking of responses to customer objections. Each objection could potentially have 30 responses, geared toward specific customer types.

- Anecdotes are persuasive writing tools – use them in your scripts. People enjoy hearing stories, especially stories that relate to them and their experiences, frustrations, and troubles. Let the story sell your product or service for you.

- Include body language in your scripts – it's just as important as your words. Try mimicking your subject's posture, arm position, and seating position. This is proven to create ease and build trust.

- If you only have your voice, use it. Pay attention to tone, language choice, speed, and background noise. You only have sound to establish a trusting relationships, so do it carefully.

- Be confident, and focus on a positive stream of self-talk to prepare for the call or presentation. Confidence sells.

- Spend time on your closing scripts, as they are a critical component of your presentation or phone call. This can be a challenging part of the sales process, so practice, practice, practice.

3

Profiting from Internet Marketing

Is your business online? If not, it should be.

The internet is today's primary consumer research tool. If your business does not have an online presence, it is harder for customers to find and choose your business over the competition. With over 73% of North Americans online, it is no wonder that individuals and businesses in all industries are looking to the internet to enhance their marketing strategies.

Luckily, it has never been easier to establish and maintain a comprehensive online presence. Internet marketing, also referred to as online marketing, online advertising or e-marketing, is the fastest growing medium for marketing.

But it is not just company websites that users are viewing. Blogs, consumer reviews, chat rooms and a variety of social media are growing rapidly in popularity.

The internet is a very powerful tool for businesses if used strategically and effectively. It can be a cost saving alternative to traditional marketing approaches, and may be the most effective way to communicate with your target consumer.

A major advantage of the internet is that you are always open. Users can access your business 24 hours a day, 7 days a week, and depending on your business and the purpose of the website, visitors can also purchase goods at any time.

Internet Marketing for Everyone

The internet is a great way to create product and brand awareness, develop relationships with consumers and share and exchange information. You can't afford not be taking advantage of online marketing opportunities because your competition is likely already there.

Internet marketing can take on many different forms. By creating maintaining a website for your business, you are reaching out to a new consumer base. You can have full control over the messaging that users are receiving and has a global reach.

Internet marketing can be very cost effective. If you have a strong email database of your customers, an e-newsletter may be cheaper and more effective than post mail. You can deliver time sensitive materials immediately and can update your subscribers instantaneously.

Top 10 Websites (Globally Jan 2017)

1.	Google	7.	Wikipedia
2.	Facebook	8.	Tencent QQ
3.	YouTube	9.	LinkedIn
4.	Windows Live	10.	Taobao.com
5.	Yahoo	11.	Twitter
6.	Baidu.com		

You will notice that half of these websites are search engines. An increasing number of consumers are first researching products, services and companies online, whether it be to compare products, complete a sale, or look for a future employer. Most people in the 18-35 age group obtain all of their information online—including news, weather, product research, etc. The remaining sites are interactive sites where users can upload information for social networking, or information sharing.

Internet Marketing Strategies

Internet marketing – like all other elements of your marketing campaign – needs to have clear goals and objectives. Creating brand and product awareness will not happen overnight so it is important to budget accordingly, ensuring there is money set aside for maintenance of the website and analytics.

Be flexible with ideas and options—do your research first, try out different options, then test and measure the results. Metrics and evaluations can be updated almost immediately and should be monitored regularly. By keeping an eye out for what online marketing strategies are working and which are not, it will be easier to create a balanced portfolio of marketing techniques. You might find that in certain geographical areas, certain marketing strategies are more effective than others.

This list is by no means the full extent of options available for marketing online, but it is a good place to start when deciding which options are best suited to your company.

Create a website

The primary use for the internet is information seeking, so you should provide consumers with information about your company first hand. You have more control over your branding and messaging and can also collect visitor information to determine what types of internet users are accessing your website.

Search Engine Optimization

Since search engines comprise 50% of the most visited sites globally, you can go through your website to make it more search engine friendly with the aim to increase your organic search listing. An organic search listing refers to listings in search engine results that appear in order or relevance to the entered search terms.

You may wish to repeat key words multiple times throughout your website and write the copy on your site not only with the end reader in mind, but also search engines.

Remember when you design your website that any text that appears in Flash format is not recognized by search engines. If your entire website is built on a Flash platform, then you will have a poor organic search listing.

Price Per Click Advertising

If you find that visitors access your website after searching for it first on a search engine, then it may be beneficial to advertise on these websites and bid on keywords associated with your company.

These advertisements will appear at the top of the page or along the left side of the search results on a search engine. You can have control over the specific geographic area you wish to target, set a monthly budget and have the option on only being charged when a user clicks on your link.

Online Directories

Listing your business in an online directory can be an inexpensive and effective online marketing strategy.

However, you need to be able to distinguish your company from the plethora of competitors that may exist. Likely, you will need to complement this strategy with other brand awareness campaigns.

Online Ads (i.e. banner ads on other websites)

These advertisements can have positive or negative effects based on the reputation and consumer perception of the website on which you are advertising. These ads should be treated similar to print ads you may place in local newspapers or other publications.

Online Videos

With the growing popularity of sites such as You Tube, it is evident that people love researching online and being able to find video clips of the information they are seeking. Depending on your small business, you may want to upload informational videos or tutorials about your products or services.

Blogging

Blogging can be a fun and interactive way to communicate with users. A blog is traditionally a website maintained by an individual user that has regular entries, similar to a diary. These entries can be commentary, descriptions of events, pictures, videos, and more. Companies can use blogging as a way to keep users updated on current information and allow them to post comments on your blog. If blogging is something you wish to invest in, make sure that it is regularly updated and monitored.

Top 10 Mistakes to Avoid

Failure to measure ROI

Which metrics are you using? Are your visitors actually motivated to purchase or sign up? If the benefits of your online campaign are not greater than the costs incurred, then you may wish to re-evaluate your strategy.

Poor Web Design

This can leave a poor impression of your company on the visitor. A poor design could result in frustration on the visitors' part if they are not able to easily find what they went on your site to search for and also does not build trust. If consumers do not trust your company or your website, you will not be able to complete the sale and develop a longer relationship with that customer. You also need to include privacy protection and security when building trust.

This also includes ensuring all information on the website is current and having customer service available if users are experiencing difficulty or cannot find the information they are seeking. This could be as simple as providing a 'Contact Us' email or phone number for support.

Becoming locked into an advertising strategy early

Remember your marketing mix when creating a marketing strategy and avoid putting all of your eggs in one basket. Online marketing is a very valuable tool, but depending on your business and your target markets, other marketing campaigns may be the best option for you. Especially if this is your first time making a significant investment into your online sector, you want to remain flexible and able to adapt your strategy based off feedback received by researching and analyzing different options.

Acting without researching

Similar to becoming locked into an advertising strategy early, this mistake implies not dutifully testing and researching different online marketing options. For example, if your target consumer is aged 65+ and you are spending all of your marketing efforts into creating a blogging website (where the average ages of bloggers are 18-35), then you are likely not going to have a successful campaign.

Assuming more visitors means more sales

You have to go back to your original goals and the purpose of your company. More visitors may not mean more sales if your website is used primarily for information and consumers purchase their products elsewhere.

This is also vice versa. You could have an increase in sales without an increase in unique visitors if your current consumer base is very loyal and willing to spend lots of money.

Often people will collect information online about products they wish to purchase because it is easier to compare options, but they purchase in person. Even though shopping online is becoming quite popular, people still prefer to see and feel the physical product before purchasing.

Failing to follow up with customers that purchase

Return sales can account for up to 60% of total revenue. It's no wonder that organizations are always trying to maintain loyal customers and may have customer relationship management systems in place. It is easier to get a happy customer to purchase again than it is to get a new customer to purchase once.

Not incorporating online marketing into the business plan

By ensuring that your online marketing plan is fully integrated and accurately represents your organization's overall goals and objectives, the business plan will be more comprehensive and encompassing.

Trying to discover your own best practices

It is very beneficial to use trial and error to determine the best online strategy from your company, but do not be afraid to do your research and learn from what other have already figured out. There will be many cases where someone was in a very similar position as you and they may have some suggestions and secrets that they wish to share. Researching in advance can save a great deal of time and money.

Spending too much too fast

Although it may be cheaper than traditional marketing approaches, internet marketing does have its costs. You have to consider the software and hardware designs, maintenance, distribution, supply chain management, and the time that will be required. You don't want to spend your entire marketing budget all at once.

Getting distracted by metrics that are not relevant

As discussed in the following section, there are endless reports and measurables that you can analyze to determine the effectiveness of your campaign. You will need to establish which measurables are actually relevant to your marketing.

Testing and Measuring Online

As with any element of your marketing campaign, you will need to track your results and measure them against your investment. Otherwise, how will you know if your online marketing is successful?

These results - or metrics – need to be recorded and analyzed as to how they impact your overall return on investment.

Some examples of metrics are:

- New account setups
- Conversion rates
- Page stickiness
- Contact us form completion

Due to the popularity in online marketing and the importance of having a strong web presence, companies have demanded more sophisticated tracking tools and metrics for their online activities. It can be very difficult to not only know what to measure, but also HOW to measure.

Thankfully, it is easier than ever to get the information you need with the many types of software and services available, including Google Analytics, which are free and relatively accurate.

8 Metrics to Track

The following are the key measurables to watch for when testing and measuring your internet marketing efforts:

Conversions

How many leads has your online presence generated, and of those leads, how many were turned into sales? Ultimately, your campaign needs to have a positive impact on your business.

Regardless of the specific purpose of the campaign – from lead generation and service sign-up, to blog entries – you need to know how many customers are taking the desired action in response to your efforts. Your tracking tool will be able to provide you with this information

Spend

If you are not making a profit – or at least breaking even – from your internet marketing efforts, then you need to change your strategy. Redistribute your financial resources and reconsider your motives and objectives for your online campaign.

An easy way to do this analysis is to divide your total spend by conversions. This could also be broken down by product. You could also use tracking tool and view reports on the 'per visit value of every click,' from every type of source. Your sources can include organic/search engine referrals, direct visit (i.e. person typed your web address into their address bar), or email/newsletter.

Attention

You need to keep a close eye on how much attention you are getting on your website. One of the best ways to analyze this would be to compare unique visitors to page views per visit to time on site. How many people are visiting, how many pages they are viewing, what pages they are viewing, and how much time they are spending on the site.

A unique visitor is any one person who visits the website in a given amount of time. For example, if Evelyn visits her online banking website daily for an entire month, over that one month period, she is considered to be one unique visitor (not 30 visitors).

You may also want to incorporate referring source as well – the places online that refer customers to your website. You'll be able to determine what referring sources offer the 'best' visitors.

Top Referrals

Know who is doing the best job of referring clients to your website – and note how they are doing this. Is it the prominence of the link? Positioning? Reputation of the referring company?

Understanding where the majority of your visitors are coming from will allow you focus on those types of sources when you increase your referral sites. They also allow you to gain a better understanding of your online market – and target audience.

Bounce Rate

The bounce rate is the number of people who visit the homepage of your website, but do not visit other pages. If you have a high bounce rate, you either have all the necessary information on your homepage, or you are not giving your customers a reason to click further.

In Google Analytics, view the 'content' or 'pages' report and view the column stating bounce rate.

Errors

It is very important to track the errors that visitors receive while trying to access or view your website. For example, if someone links to your website, but makes a spelling error in typing the link, your users will see an error page in their browser, and will not ultimately make it to your website.

You can also receive reports on errors that customer's make when trying to type in your website address in their browser. You may wish to buy the domains with common spelling mistakes, and link those addresses to you true homepage. This will increase overall traffic and potential conversions.

Onsite Search Terms

If you have a 'search website' function on your website, it is useful to monitor which terms users are most frequently searching. This can provide valuable insight into the user friendliness of your site and your website's navigation system. This information will be included in the traffic reporting tool.

Bailout Rates

If you provide users with the option to purchase something on your website (i.e. shopping cart), then you can track where along the purchasing process people decided not to go through with the sale.

This could be at the first step of receiving the order summary and total, or further when stating shipping options. By obtaining this information, a company can reorganize or revamp their website to make the sales process more fluid and possibly encourage more purchases.

Here are the three main questions you should be asking yourself when evaluating your website presence:

- o   Who visits my website?
- o   Where do visitors come from?
- o   Which pages are viewed?

4

How to Profit from Direct Mail

Every time you mail an existing or potential customer a letter and ask them to respond or take action, you are running a direct-mail campaign.

Direct mail is a marketing strategy that can help you achieve a number of business objectives. From lead generation to customer retention, direct mail campaigns are a highly versatile and relatively cost-effective choice for business promotion.

What you probably don't realize is that direct mail is one of the most targeted marketing strategies you can implement, and one of the easiest to track, measure and analyze results.

It is also one of the most personal. Instead of an advertisement, flyer, newspaper insert or catalogue, you are sending each customer a personalized letter that is tailored to their unique needs and desires.

Getting the most out of your direct mail campaign is easy. With a laser-sharp mailing list and irresistible offer, your direct mail campaign can easily flood your business with qualified leads.

Let's get started!

A List of Ideal Customers

Unless you spend time carefully crafting a mailing list of ideal customers, you may as well pack and up go home. The success of a direct mail campaign largely rests on the pinpoint accuracy of your mailing list.

The only people you want on your list are your potential "ideal customers." The people who are most likely to buy from you – often and in large volumes – and who are a delight to deal with. They are the type of people who will account for 80% of your revenue, and just 20% of your total customer base.

You have a number of options when you are creating your mailing list:

- **Existing customer database**. This is a list of all of the people who have previously purchased from you. It is important to gather their full contact information at the time of sale so you will be able to get contact them again.

- **Existing leads database**. This is a list of all of the leads that have come through your door, but have not purchased from you. This may include those who responded to your last direct mail campaign, but have not yet become customers.

- **Outsourced list**. This is a list that has been purchased from a market research firm, the government, or the post office. These lists are pulled based on demographic information – age, sex, location, income, family structure, etc.

Putting the mailing list together

Once you have determined the source(s) for your mailing list, you will have to spend some time assembling it and preparing it for your mailing.

1. Make sure all contacts are up to date. Phone old contacts to confirm their mailing address. An out-of-date list will cost you money in printing and postage.

2. Ensure all contacts are accurate to the list criteria. Take a read through your list to make sure there are no contacts that shouldn't be on the list.

3. Use a database management program to manage your mailing. This will allow you to keep a master list, and create custom lists for each mailing. Remember to save the file name as something that describes the mailing so you can easily find it.

Writing Effective Direct Mail Pieces

Now that you have a laser-sharp mailing list, you will want to do everything you can to target your message to the recipients on your list.

An effective direct mail piece:

- **Has a clear structure.** The piece is clearly a letter – there is an engaging headline, clear message, point form list of benefits, and postscript.

- **Features an irresistible offer.** The purchase opportunity is too good for the target audience to refuse. It includes an element of scarcity and urgency.

- **Focuses on customer benefits.** The customer clearly understands "what's in it for me?" The product or service is clearly positioned as something of value and a solution to a need, problem, or desire.

- **Is personal and conversational.** The letter is personally addressed, and reads as though it was composed specifically for the recipient. It is written in conversational tone, with short sentences and limited description.

- **Is short.** The letter communicates what it needs to, and closes. It does not go on for pages in length. The messages are clear, succinct, and simple.

- **Is urgent.** The piece gives the reader to act immediately. There is a time limit or a quantity limit to the offer that requires an urgent response.

- **Includes a Postscript.** The offer or urgency is repeated after the signature at the bottom of the letter. Like a headline, everyone will read the P.S.

The Five-Step Direct Mail Campaign

1. Determine Your Target Audience

As we discussed above, you will want to ensure that you have the most accurate, targeted list possible for your direct mail campaign.

Be clear about the purpose for your direct mail campaign – this will help you decide if you want to send your letters to your entire target market, a segment of that market, existing customers, or potentially a referring business's customers. Then you can determine how you craft your offer, how you structure your letter, and when you choose to send it.

2. Choose what you want to say

What is the message you want to communicate to your target list? What can you offer them that will entice them to act immediately?

Create a specific offer for each direct mail campaign to ensure each time you communicate with your target list you have something new to say. Tailor this offer to each mailing list.

Decide what product or service benefits will be most compelling to your target audience, and include those benefits prominently in your letter.

3. Develop a compelling direct mail piece

You are in control of how your format your message. Are you sending a letter? A brochure and a letter? A postcard? The format of your direct mail piece needs to be tailored to your target list, and reflect your product or service. A younger audience may respond to a postcard, but an older audience may appreciate a formalized letter.

Ensure that whatever format you choose, the piece is professionally designed, prominently includes your logo and company branding, and is professionally produced.

This piece of paper has to act as an ambassador of your company – you absolutely need it to appear impressive and professional.

4. Pick your timing

Some products and purchase decisions are best made at certain times of the year, or the month. If your business or service is seasonal, then there are good times and bad times to try to generate leads. Consider the best purchase windows for the people in your target marketing. When do they get paid? When do they have the money to spend on your product/service? When do they spend the most money?

Anticipate these windows, and time your direct mail campaign accordingly. If you run a lawn sprinkler installation system and summer is your peak season, run a direct mail campaign mid-way through spring, and at the beginning of summer.

Some common time windows include:

- Holiday season (November – December)
- Fridays (paydays)
- The 15th and 30th of every months (also paydays)
- Seasons (Spring, Summer, Fall, Winter)
- Financial cycles (year-end, tax time)
- Sports seasons (hockey, football, baseball, etc.)

5. Follow up

Comprehensive follow up to a direct mail campaign means two things:

1. Following up on your letter with a phone call or second letter

Often it takes more than a letter to get a potential customer to take action. This can be a result of the accuracy of your mailing list, your offer, the time of the year, or the quality of the marketing material (brochure). If you are certain that your mailing list is accurate and up to date, follow up to the piece with a phone call, or send another letter.

2. Recording, measuring and analyzing your results.

It is essential that you evaluate each direct mail campaign based on your time and financial investment and your rate of response. How else will you be able to tell if it was a successful or effective strategy?

For each campaign, record and analyze the following information:

- Number of letters sent
- Number or responses as a percentage
- Number of sales directly resulting from the campaign
- Number of enquiries
- Total value of sales directly resulting from the campaign

Based on this information, determine if the campaign was successful (did it make you money?) or not. Consider making some changes to your list, your offer, or the piece itself, and try again.

5

Systemizing Your Business and Developing Effective Processes

One of the biggest mistakes a business owner can make is to create a company that is dependent on the owner's involvement for the success of its daily operations. This is called working "in" your business. You're writing basic sales letters, licking stamps, and guiding staff step-by-step through each task.

There are a number of problems with this approach. One is redundancy. You're paying your staff to carry out tasks that you eventually complete. The second is poor time management. You're spending your day – at your high hourly rate – on tasks as they arise, leaving little room for the tasks you need to be focused on.

However, the biggest issue I have with this approach is that countless intelligent business owners are spending the majority of their time operating their business, instead of *growing* it.

A good test of this is to ask yourself, what would happen if you took off to a hot sunny destination for three weeks and left your cell phone, PDA and laptop at home. Would your business be able to continue operating?

If you said no, then this chapter is for you.

Systemizing your business is about putting policies and procedures in place to make your business operations run smoother – and more importantly – without your constant involvement. With your newfound free time, **you will be able to focus your efforts on the bigger picture: strategically growing your business.**

Why Systemize?

For most small business owners, systems simply mean freedom from the day-to-day functioning of their organization. The company runs smoothly, makes a profit, and provides a high level of service – regardless of the owner's involvement.

Systemizing your business is also a healthy way to plan for the future. You're not going to be working forever – what happens when you retire? How will you transition your business to new ownership or management? How will you take that vacation you've been dreaming of?

Businesses that function without their ownership are also highly valuable to investors. Systemizing your business can position it in a favorable light for purchase, and merit a high price tag.

A system is any process, policy, or procedure that consistently achieves the same result, regardless of who is completing the task.

Any task that is performed in your business more than once can be systemized. Ideally, the tasks that are completed on a cyclical basis – daily, weekly, monthly, and quarterly – should be systemized so much so that anyone can perform them.

Systems can take many forms – from manuals and instruction sheets, to signs, banners, and audio or video recordings. They don't have to be elaborate or extensive, just provide enough information in step-by-step form to guide the person performing the task.

Benefits of Business Systems

There are unlimited benefits available to you and your business through systemization. The more systems you can successfully implement, the more benefits you'll see.

- Better cost management
- Improved time management
- Clearer expectations of staff
- More effective staff training and orientation
- Increased productivity (and potentially profits)
- Happier customers (consistent service)
- Maximized conversion rates
- Increased staff respect for your time
- Increased level of individual initiative
- Greater focus on long-term business growth

Taking Stock of Your Existing Systems

The first step in systemizing your business is taking a long look at the existing systems (if any) in your business. At this point, you can look for any systems that have simply emerged as "the way we do things here."

How do your staff answer the phone? What is the process customers go through when dealing with your business? How are employees hired? Trained? How is performance Reviewed and rewarded?

Some of your systems may be highly effective, and not require any changes. Others may be ineffective and require some reworking. If you have previously established some systems, now is a good time to check-in and evaluate how well they are functioning.

Use the following chart to record what systems currently exist in your business.

Existing Systems	
Administration	
Financials	

Communication	
Customer Relations	
Employees	
Marketing	
Data	

Seven Areas to Systemize

There is no doubt that system creation – especially when none exist to begin with – is a daunting and time-consuming task. For many businesses, it can be difficult to determine where to start to make the best use of their time from the onset.

Here are seven main areas of your business you can to systemize. Begin with one area, and move to the other areas as you are ready. Alternately, start with one or two systems within each area, and evaluate how those new systems affect your business. Each business will require its own unique set of systems.

1. Administration

This is an important area of your business to systemize because administrative roles tend to see a high turnover. A series of systems will reduce training time, and keep you from explaining how the phones are to be answered each time a new receptionist joins your team.

Administrative Systems	
Opening and closing procedures	Filing and paper management
Phone greeting	Workflow
Mail processing	Document production
Sending couriers	Inventory management
Office maintenance (watering plants, emptying recycle bins, etc.)	Order processing
	Making orders

2. Financials

This is one area of systems that you will need to keep a close eye on – but that doesn't mean you have to do the work yourself. Financial management systems are everything from tracking credit card purchases to invoicing clients and following up on overdue accounts.

These systems will help to prevent employee theft, and allow you to always have a clear picture of your numbers. It will allow you to control purchasing, and ensure that each decision is signed-off on.

Financial Systems	
Purchasing	Profit / loss statements
Credit card purchase tracking	Invoicing
Accounts payable	Daily cash out
Accounts receivable	Petty cash
Bank deposits	Employee expenses
Cutting checks	Payroll
Tax payments	Commission payments

3. Communications

The area of communication is essential and time consuming for any business. Fax cover letters, sales letters, internal memos, reports, and newsletters are items that need to be created regularly by different people in your organization.

Most of the time, these communications aren't much different from one to the next, yet each are created from scratch by a different person. There is a huge opportunity for systemization in this area of your business. Systemized communication ensures consistency and company differentiation.

Communication Systems	
Internal memo template	Newsletter template
Fax cover template	Sales letter template(s)
Letterhead template	Meeting minutes template
Team meeting agenda	Report template
Sending faxes	Internal meetings
Internal emails	Scheduling

4. Customer Relations

Another important area for systemization is customer relations. This includes everything the customer sees or touches in your company, as well as any interaction they might have with you or your staff members.

Establishing a customer relations system will also ensure that new staff members understand how customers are handled in *your* business. It will allow you to maintain a high level of customer service, without constantly reminding staff of your policies. It will also ensure that the success of your customer relations and retention does not hinge on you or any other individual salesperson.

Customer Relations Systems	
Incoming phone call script	Sales process
Outgoing phone call script	Sales script
Customer service standards	Newsletter templates
Customer retention strategy	Ongoing customer communication strategy
Customer communications templates	
	Customer liaison policy

5. Employees

Create systems in your business for hiring, training, and developing your employees. This will establish clear expectations for the employee, and streamline time consuming activities like recruitment.

Employees with clear expectations who work within clear structures are happier and more productive. They are motivated to achieve 'A' when they know they will receive 'B' if they do. Establishing a clear training manual will also save you and your staff the time and hassle of training each new staff member on the fly.

Employee Systems	
Employee recruitment	Staff uniforms or dress code
Employee retention	Employee training
Incentive and rewards program	Ongoing training and professional development
Regular employee reviews	
Employee feedback structure	Job descriptions and role profiles

6. Marketing

This is likely an area in which you spend a large part of your time. You focus on generating new leads and getting more people to call you or walk through your doors. These efforts can be systemized and delegated to other staff members.

Use the information in this program to create simple systems for your basic promotional efforts. Any one of your staff should be able to pick up a marketing manual and implement a successful direct mail campaign or place a purposeful advertisement.

Marketing Systems	
Referral program	Regular advertisements
Customer retention program	Advertisement creation system
Regular promotions	Direct mail system
Marketing calendar	Sales procedures
Enquiries management	Lead management

7. Data

While we like to think we operate a paperless office, often the opposite is true. Your business needs to have clear systems for managing paper and electronic information to ensure that information is protected, easily accessed, and only kept when necessary.

Data management systems help you keep your office organized. Everyone knows where information is to be stored, and how it is to be handled, which prevents big stacks of paper with no place to go.

Ensure that within your data management systems you include a data backup system. That way, if anything happens to you server or computer software, your data – and potentially your business – is protected.

Data Management Systems	
IT Management	Client file system
Data backup	Project file system
Computer repairs	Point of sale system
Electronic information storage	Financial data management

Implementing New Systems

If you completed the exercise earlier in this chapter, you will have a good idea of the systems that are currently in place in your business. The next step is to determine what systems you need to create in your business.

To do this you will need to get a better understanding of the tasks that you and your employees complete on a daily and weekly basis. If you operate a timesheet program, this can be a good source of information. Alternately, ask staff to keep a daily log for a week of all the tasks they contribute to or complete. Doing so will not only give you valuable insight into their how they spend their time on a daily basis, but also involve them in the systemizing process.

Review all task logs or timesheet records at the end of the week, remove duplicates, and group like tasks together. From here you can categorize the tasks into business areas like the seven listed above, or create your own categories.

Then, you will need to prioritize and plan your system creation and implementation efforts. Choose one from each category, or one category to focus on at a time. The amount you can take on will depend on your business needs, and the staff resources you have available to you for this process.

Remember that system creation is a long-term process – not something that will transform your business overnight. Be patient, and focus on the items that hold the highest priority.

Creating Your Systems

There is a big variety of ways you can create systems for your business – depending on the type of system you need and the type of business you operate. Some systems will be short and simple – i.e., a laminated sign in the kitchen that outlines step-by-step how to make the coffee – while others will be more complex – i.e., your sales scripts or letter templates.

One thing all of your systems have in common is steps. There is a linear process involved from start to finish. Begin by writing out each of the steps involved in completing the task, and provide as much detail as you can.

Then, review your step-by-step guide with the employee(s) who regularly complete the task and gather their feedback. Once you have incorporated their input, decide what format the system needs to be in: manual, laminated instruction sheet, sign, office memo, etc.

Testing Your Systems

Now that you have created a system, you will need to make sure that it works. More specifically, you need to make sure that it works without your involvement.

Implement the new system for an appropriate period of time – a week or month – then ask for input from staff, suppliers and vendors, and customers. Evaluate if it is informative enough for your staff, seamless enough for your suppliers, and whether or not it meets or exceeds your customer's needs.

Take that feedback and revise the system accordingly. You will rarely get the system right the first time – so be patient.

Systems will also need to be evaluated and revised on a regular basis to ensure your business processes are kept up to date. Structure an annual or bi-annual review of systems, and stick to it.

Employee Buy-In

It will be nearly impossible for you to develop effective systems without the involvement and input of your employees. These are the people who will be using the systems, and who are completing the tasks on a regular basis without systems. They have a wealth of knowledge to assist you in this process.

Employees can also draft the systems for you to review and finalize. This will make the systemization process a much faster and more efficient one.

It is also important to note that when you introduce new systems into your company, there may be a natural resistance to the change. People – including your employees – are habitual people who can become set in the way they are used to doing things.

Delegation

The final step to systemizing your business is delegation. What is the point of creating systems unless someone other than you can use them to perform tasks?

This doesn't have to mean completely removing your involvement from the process, but it does mean giving your employees enough freedom to complete the task within the structure of the systems you have spent time and considerable thought creating.

After that, allow yourself the freedom of focusing on the tasks that you most enjoy, and most deserve your time – like creating big picture strategies to grow your business and increase your profits.

6

How to Double your Referrals

What if I told you that you could put an inexpensive system in place that would effectively allow your business to growth itself?

For most business owners, a large part of their customer base is comprised of referral customers. These people found out about the company's products or services from the recommendation of a friend or colleague who had a positive experience purchasing from that company.

If your business benefits from referral customers, you will find that these customers arrive ready to buy from you, and tend to buy more often. They also tend to be highly loyal to your product or service.

Seem like great customers to have, don't they?

Referral customers cost less to acquire. Compared to the leads you generate from advertising, direct mail campaigns, and other marketing initiatives, referral customers come to you already qualified and already trusting in the quality of your offering and the respectability of your staff.

With a little effort, and the creation of a formalized system – or strategy – you can not only continue to enjoy referral business, but easily double the number of referral customers that walk through your door. All of this is possible for a minimal investment of time and resources.

Is Your Business a Referral Business?

Referral based businesses benefit from a stream of qualified customers who arrive at their doorstep ready to spend. These businesses put less focus on advertising to generate new leads, and more focus on serving and communicating with their existing customers.

Generally speaking, a referral program can generate outstanding results for nearly any business. Since most referrals do not require any effort, the addition of a strategy and a program will often double or triple the number of qualified referrals that come through a business door.

There are, however, a few types of businesses that will not benefit from a formalized referral strategy. These are businesses with low price points – like fast food restaurants and drugstores. Their customer base is large already, and their efforts would be best spent on increasing the average sale.

A referral program can:

- **Save you time**. Referral strategies – once established – don't require much management or time investment.

- **Deliver more qualified customers**. Your customer arrives with an assumption of trust, and willing to purchase.

- **Improve your reputation.** Your customer's networks likely overlap, and create potential for a single customer to be referred by two people. This encourages the perception that your business is "the place to go."

- **Speed the sales process.** You will have existing common ground and a reputation with the referred customer.

- **Increase your profit.** You will spend less time and money generating leads, and more time serving customers who have their wallets open.

The Cost of Your Customers

As we discussed in the "Repeat Business" section, you don't "get" customers, you *buy* them. The money you spend on advertising, direct mail, and other promotions ideally results in potential customers walking through your doors.

For example, if you placed an ad for $200, and 20 people make a purchase in response to that ad, you would have paid $10 for each customer.

Referral customers cost you next to nothing. Your existing customer does the work of selling your business to their friend or associate, and you benefit from the sale. Aside from the cost of any referral incentives or coupon production, there is no cost involved at all.

Referral customers cost less and require less time investment than any other customer. That means you can spend that time making them a loyal customer, or a devoted fan.

Groom Your Customers

Referral strategies can allow you to groom your customer base. As we have previously discussed, 80% of your revenue comes from 20% of your customers – these are your ideal customers.

These are also the people you have established as your target market, and are the people you cater your marketing and advertising efforts toward.

You also have a group of customers who make up 80% of your headaches. These are the people who complain the most and spend the least.

Use your referral strategy to get more of your *ideal* customers. Spend more time servicing your ideal customers – do everything you can to make them happy – and less time on your headache customers. You can even ask your headache customers to shop elsewhere.

Then, focus your referral efforts on your ideal customers. Ask them to refer business to you, and reward them for doing so. Try to avoid referrals from your headache customers – chances are you'll just get another headache.

Referral Sources

Take some time to brainstorm all the people who could potentially refer business to you. Think beyond your business, to your extracurricular activities and personal life. There are endless sources of people who are ready and willing to send potential customers your way.

Here are some ideas to get you started:

Past Relationships

No, not romantic relationships. I'm talking about anyone you have previously had a relationship with, but for one reason or another have fallen out of touch. This includes former colleagues, associates, customers and friends.

Including them in your referral strategy can be as simple as reaching out through the phone or email, and updating them on your latest business initiative or career move. Gently ask at the end of the correspondence to refer anyone who may need your product or service. They will appreciate that you have attempted to re-establish the relationship.

Suppliers and Vendors

Your suppliers and vendors can be a great source for referrals, because they presumably deal daily with businesses that are complementary to your own. The opportunities to connect two of their customers in a mutually beneficial relationship are endless. These businesses should be happy to help out - especially if you have been a regular and loyal customer.

Customers

Customers are an obvious source of referrals because they are the people who are dealing with you directly on a regular basis. Often, all you have to do is ask and they will happily provide you with contact information of other interested buyers, or contact those buyers themselves.

Your customers also have a high level of product knowledge when it comes to your business, and are in a great position to really sell the strength of your company. Remember from the Testimonials section, the words of your customers are at least 10 times more powerful than any clever headline or marketing piece you could create.

Employees and Associates

Give your employees and associates a reason to have their friends and families shop at your business with a simple incentive program. These people have the most product knowledge, and are in the best position to sell you to a potential customer.

This is also a way to tap into an endless network of people. Who do your employees and associates know? Who do their friends and friends of friends know? A referral chain that connects to your employees can be a highly powerful one.

Competitors

This doesn't seem so obvious, but it can work. Your direct competitors are clearly not the ideal source for referrals. However, indirect competitors can refer their clients or potential clients to you if they cannot meet those clients' needs themselves.

For example, if you sell high end lighting fixtures, the low-budget lighting store down the street may be able to refer clients to you, and vice versa. You may wish to offer a finder's fee or incentive to establish this arrangement.

Your Network

Don't be shy about asking your friends and family members for referrals. Too many people do not provide enough information to their inner circle about what they do or what their business does. This doesn't make sense, since these are the people who should be the most interested!

Take time to explain clearly what your business is all about, and what your point of difference is. Then just ask them if they know anyone who may benefit from what you are offering. You could even provide your friends and family with an incentive – a gift, a meal, or a portion of the sale.

Associations + Special Interest Groups

This is another place you likely have a network of people who have limited knowledge about what you do or what your business does. The advantage here is that you have a group of people with similar belief s and values in the same room. Use it!

The Media

Unless a member of the media is a regular customer of yours, or you are in business to serve the media, this may not seem like an obvious choice either.

The opportunity here is to establish a relationship with an editor or journalist, and position yourself as an expert in your field or industry. Then, next time they are writing a related story, they can ask to quote you and your opinion. When their audience reads the story, they will perceive your business as the industry leader.

Referral Strategies

A referral strategy is any system you can put in place to generate new leads through existing customers. The ideal way to do this is to create a system that runs itself! Here are some ideas for simple strategies you can begin to implement into your business immediately.

Just Ask

This may seem simple and obvious, but it's true. Be open with your customers and associates, and simply ask them if they can refer any of their friends or associates to you. Make it part of doing business with you, and your customers will grow to expect the question. Or, let them know in advance that you'll be asking at a later date.

Remember that this can include potential customers – even if they don't buy from you. The reason they chose not to purchase may have nothing to do with your business; any person who has begun to or actually done business with you can refer to you another person.

Offer Incentives

When you speak to your customers, when you ask them for something, you typically try to answer the question "what's in it for me?" before they ask it.

The same is true when you ask your customers for a referral. Incentive-based referral strategies work wonders, and can easily be implemented as part of a customer loyalty program, or as part of your existing customer relations systems.

Consider offering customers who successfully refer clients to you discounts on products, free products or services, or gifts. Offer incentives relative to the number of referrals, or the success rate of each referral.

This can have a spin off effect, as your referral customers may become motivated to continue the referral chain. They too will be interested in the incentives you have provided, and tell their friends about your business.

Be Proactive

The only way your referral program will work is if you put some effort into it, and maintain some level of ongoing effort.

Here are some ideas:

- Put a referral card or coupon in every shopping bag that leaves your store
- Promote gift certificates during peak seasons
- Offer free information seminars to existing customers, and ask them to bring a friend
- Host a closed-door sale for your top 20 customers and their friends

Provide Great Customer Service

An easy way to encourage referral business is to treat every potential customer with exemplary customer service. Since the art of customer service is lost is many communities, people are often impressed by simple added touches and conveniences. That alone will encourage them to refer your business to their network.

Stay in Touch

Make sure you are staying in touch with all of your potential and converted customers. Through newsletters, direct mail, or the Internet, keep your business name at the top of the minds, ahead of the competition.

Even if they have already purchased from you, and may not need to purchase for some time, a newsletter or email can be a simple reminder that your business is out there. If someone in their network is looking for the product or service, it will be more likely that your customer will refer your business over the competition.

7

Staff Recruitment Training and Development

The people you hire to work for your business can be your biggest assets and your biggest headaches. They can support and help you to achieve the vision you have for your company – but they can also prevent you from reaching that vision.

Too many businesses overlook the role of employee recruitment and retention when planning for the success of their organization. Staffing is an important exercise that needs to be purpose driven and strategic, just like marketing.

It is vital to understand in today's market that the relationship between employee and employer is a two-way street. Now, more than ever, employees have a "what's in it for me?" attitude that extends beyond salary and benefits expectations into incentive and rewards programs. The days of simple compensation structures are over.

Now, this may sound like a big headache, but it's actually a good thing! With some simple systems and open dialogue, you will be able to effectively create – and keep – your dream team.

The Power of Your Dream Team

How much of your own personal time has human resources – staff hiring, firing, issues management, etc. – taken this year? No doubt staff recruitment and retention is one of the biggest challenges facing any business owner today.

The truth is, if you spent half as much time on human resources as you do on marketing, I guarantee your sales would increase dramatically.

Customers know the difference between happy employees and disgruntled ones, and it makes a difference when it comes to purchase decisions. Would you rather have your car serviced by a grumpy mechanic who doesn't feel his good work is rewarded, or a pleasant one who just stepped out a weekly team meeting?

A successful business owner has confidence in the people who work for him, because he believes they are the best people for the job. Employees who know their employer believes in their skills and abilities will go over and above to get the job done, to make the sale.

Successful business owners invest time and money in finding and keeping the right people. These are the people who share and support the collective vision for the company.

I'm not talking about a complicated formula, or magic concoction. I'm talking about some careful thought and a proactive strategy that will make your business shine from the inside out.

Finding Your Dream Employees

Building a dream team starts by finding and hiring the right people for the job. Sounds simple enough. You post an ad, find someone who has the necessary qualifications, and hire them on.

Not so fast. Recruitment is complex process that can dramatically impact your business operations. Just like finding and securing the right customers, finding and hiring the right candidates requires pro-active planning and careful evaluation.

If you currently work with a recruiting agency to build to your team, now may be a good time to stop and evaluate the effectiveness of their service. While a recruiting agency can save you the time and hassle of working through the hiring process, it can also cost more money in the long run.

I always recommend creating an internal recruitment system, not because recruiting agencies do a bad job, but because no one knows your business like you do.

An internal recruitment system ensures that the true essence of your business culture is communicated – from advertisement to interview. You also have the opportunity to communicate expectations from the outset, instead of relying on the recruiter to relay this information. The middle-man's thoughts and impressions are eliminated, leaving you to make decisions based on your impression of the candidate and no one else's.

Step One: Advertise the Opportunity

The first step in recruiting candidates is obviously letting potential candidates know about the opportunity with your company.

But before you pick up the phone to place a classified ad, remember that advertising for potential employees requires just as much consideration and planning as general advertising for your business.

You need to ask yourself:

- Who is your ideal candidate?
- What are their skills and qualifications?
- What is their personality or demeanor?
- What are they passionate about?
- What are they looking for in a job?

Once you have a mental picture of your candidate, then you can begin to write an ad that will not only reach them, but also inspire them to act (and submit an application).

When writing this ad, be as specific as possible and focus on the benefits of the job. Remember that potential candidates screen job postings with an eye for "what's in it for me." Tell them exactly that.

Here are a few sample job postings:

Are you the Marketing Assistant we need?

About You

You're fun, friendly and have a keen eye for detail. You're always two steps ahead of your colleagues, and eager to take on new and exciting challenges.

You'll be the glue that keeps the marketing team operating in a seamless fashion, responsible for website updates, copywriting, event coordination and client relations. You'll be punctual, responsible, and well put together.

You'll ideally have an undergraduate degree in marketing or English, and some previous office experience, but a fast learner with a great attitude will also get our attention.

About Us

We are a collaborate team of young professionals. We offer a competitive salary, great benefits and performance incentives.

Think you fit the bill? Email your resume and cover letter to John Smith at jsmith@email.com by Friday at 4pm.

Are Computers Your Life?

About You

You are smart, outgoing, and a wiz when it comes to computer programming. You're on your friend's speed dial for computer emergencies, large and small. Helping people understand the complex digital world is your passion.

You'll be our Lead Computer Technician, managing our computer repair counter and five Junior Technicians. You'll have great people skills, mounds of patience, and enjoy working as part of a dynamic team.

About Us

We operate Anytown's leading computer repair store, and are known across the region for our customer service. We work hard, play hard, and offer a competitive benefits package to our employees.

Tell us why this job is for you. Email your resume and cover letter to info@computerworld.com by Thursday, September 23.

Both of these job postings speak directly to a very targeted audience. They're friendly, colloquial, and communicate the job requirements in an informal way.

Every job posting should:

- Be colloquial (written in the way that you talk)
- Be specific
- Describe benefits
- Include skills, qualifications, duties and job title
- Be written in the present tense
- Have a great headline
- Call the reader to action
- Be simple – in word choice and sentence structure
- Be more exciting than the competition

Now that you have a great ad to post, you need to decide where you are going to publish it. This depends on the level of the job (junior to management) and on the specific type of candidate you are looking to recruit.

Here are the five major places to advertise your opportunity:

Government Employment Center

These are great places to find blue-collar or junior level employees. Candidates register with the center, which keeps their resumes on file. Be cautious with this route – it can produce a wide variety of candidates who are not qualified.

Local Newspaper

This is a great place to post junior to mid-level employment opportunities. You're looking for basic qualifications from local applicants, perhaps even for part-time positions, with minimal cost.

Regional or City Newspaper

Senior employment opportunities that require specific high-level qualifications are best advertised with a broad scope. This incurs a greater cost, but will return a greater variety of candidates.

Online

This is a cheap way to tap into a massive database of job seekers. Post your ad online on sites like www.monster.com or www.workopolis.com and watch the resumes come flooding in. A large number of highly qualified job seekers who do not wish to register with a recruitment agency will use these services.

Referrals

The most ideal way to find candidates is through your existing network – including associates, colleagues, employees, friends and family. These candidates come to you already vetted by a trusted source. You may also wish to consider giving your staff an incentive to refer their qualified friends and associates to you.

You should also brainstorm a list of any other niche areas that your target market may look for a job. Consider industry publications, industry associations, small publications, etc.

Once you've posted your ad, your next step is to manage the inquiries that come flooding in.

Step Two: Screen Candidates

This is one of the most time-consuming aspects of the recruitment process, so you will need to work out a system to manage the response to your job posting.

A system will also allow you ensure you ask all potential candidates the same questions, and provide them with the same information about the role as well as about your company.

1. Decide whether all inquiries will be handled by one person or several. This will depend on your staff resources and capacity. A system will allow multiple employees to assist in the process.

For example, if your candidates have been instructed to submit their resume and cover letter to you through email, designate a single email address and inbox to receiving and responding. This way you or another staff member will not be bombarded by emails, and can designate an hour of time each day to managing the inquiries. If your candidates are calling in, designate a unique phone number or answering machine to this purpose.

2. Decide how inquiries will be responded to. This can be as simple as an email acknowledging receipt of the resume, or specific instructions on an answering machine. Ensure everyone receives the same information, and that you receive the same level of information from all candidates (resume, cover letter, portfolio, references, and other relevant information.).

If you have asked candidates to call you instead of submit their resumes through email, create a standard checklist of questions to ask them, as well as of information to provide them with. You may wish to create a script. Some questions might include:

- What kind of job are you looking for?
- Why do you think you would be well suited to this position?
- Tell me a bit about yourself.
- What makes you interested in our company?

Use this opportunity to get a feel for the applicant's personality, and trust your initial impression. Create a form on which to record this information, and file it with their resume when you receive it.

3. Devise a process for reviewing resumes or applications. The easiest and most time efficient way to do this is in a single session, after the stated deadline, and not as you receive them. You may wish to enlist the assistance of a senior colleague to provide a second opinion.

Review the resumes and application materials, and divide the applications into three piles: interview, no interview, and maybe. From here you can begin to call candidates and set up a first interview.

It is also a good idea to be in touch with unsuccessful candidates, and politely let them know that you will not be asking them in for an interview. If you anticipate your response rate will be overwhelming, you may wish to consider stating in your advertisement that only successful applicants will be called.

Step Three: First Interview

The first interview is also a screening interview; your objective is to develop a first impression of the candidate as a person, and to determine if they are qualified for the position. If you feel you have found an ideal candidate, this is also your opportunity to convince them to choose your company over any others they may be considering. Good people don't stay in the market long.

Interview Structure

You will need to decide on a structure, or system, for the interview process as well. Will you be conducting the first interviews, or will another manager? Will the interviews be conducted one on one, or will several employees participate? If you are replacing an employee, you may want to consider inviting that employee into the interview to provide insight into the role.

Interview Materials

Just as you are asking the potential candidate to come prepared to the interview, you must be as well.

- Have an outline prepared of what you would like to cover. Topics include: company history, job description, interview questions, compensation structure, availability, and room for advancement.
- Bring two copies of a typed job description. Include all tasks the candidate will be responsible for completing or assisting with.
- A company profile or overview document (other marketing collateral will also work here).

Interview Attitude

Begin to build a relationship with each applicant. The purpose of the interview is not just to discuss the job description, or for the applicant to get all the interview questions "right." It is to determine if this person has the right attitude for the job, and whether or not they will fit in with the company's culture and its employees.

Keep the interview professional, but make sure the applicant is comfortable. Interviews test our ability to perform under pressure, but you will want to gain an understanding of the applicant's true nature. Remember that even if the applicant is not well suited to the role they have applied for, they may be suited to a future opportunity with the company.

Interview Questions

The questions you decide to ask the candidate are highly specific to your company and the role you are hiring for. Take some time to brainstorm what you really need to know about each person, and what questions you can ask to get that information.

Keep in mind that part of the objective of the first interview is to get a sense of the candidate's personality. You will want to ask questions about their responses, and begin to establish a real relationship with them.

Here are some starter interview questions to get you going:

- Tell me a little bit about your background.
- What has been your first impression of our company/product/services?
- Tell me about a time when...[insert a likely scenario they will encounter in the position]. How did it make you feel? How did you handle the situation?
- What advantages do you feel you have over the other candidates?
- What are your strengths? Weaknesses?
- Tell me about an achievement you're proud of.
- Why did you leave your last position?
- Where do you see yourself in five years?
- ...and so on.

Make sure you take good notes, or ask a junior member of your team to take notes for you. Also record your impression of the candidate after each interview. You will want to be able to reflect on each interview before inviting the candidate to the next phase of the selection process.

When the first interviews have been completed, review your notes and discuss your first impressions with other employees involved in the process. Then, decide who you would like to invite back for a second interview, and let the unsuccessful candidates know they are not right for this particular role.

Step Four: Second Interview + Reference Check

The second interview is used to confirm your impressions of the applicants you believe are well suited to the job. It can also be used to get more information, or to more closely compare two solid candidates.

Make sure you only offer a second interview to those you are considering hiring. If you are on the fence about a candidate, chances are your instincts are right, and bringing them in for a second interview is a waste of their time and yours.

Callbacks

When you call a candidate to invite them to come in for a second interview, remain professional and don't make any allusions to a job offer. If your impression of them changes during the second interview, you do not want to have to go back on something you said. Let them know what you thought of them based on the first interview, and ask if they would be interested in meeting with you a second time.

Give yourself and the candidate at day or two between interviews to reflect on the first interview and prepare for the second.

Interviewer

You may wish to change the person or team of people who conducted the first interview. Usually the second interview is conducted with more senior team members at the table.

Interview Questions

While the second interview is often less structured than the first – a relationship has already begun to be established – you should still prepare a list of questions for the candidate.

These questions should focus on the specific tasks related to the job, and on providing more information about the culture, systems, and values of the company. You can also use the second interview to ask questions you may not have had the chance to in the first interview.

Office Tour + Introductions

Once you have determined that you have found the candidate for the job, take them on a tour of your office or business, and introduce them to your staff members. This is a good way gaining an initial understanding of how the candidate might interact with your existing staff members.

Calling References

This is the final – arguably most important – step to make before offering the job to the candidate. You should ask your candidate for at least three employment references, and perhaps one character reference.

Call each reference contact, and explain who you are and why you are calling. Then ask if they have a few moments to answer some questions about the candidate. You will want to find out information about punctuality, professionalism, skills, and their reason for leaving. Cross reference this information with your interview notes to ensure consistency between the candidate and their reference.

Step Five: Hire Your Employee

Provided their references are solid, now is the time to make them an offer of employment.

Call the candidate personally to offer them the job. Make sure you congratulate them, and express your enthusiasm in welcoming them into your team. You will also need to follow up your conversation with a letter or email that includes the job offer document or contract.

In the case a candidate declines the job offer, you may wish to do a reference check on your second pick candidate and make them an offer.

Good luck!

Training Your Dream Employees

Once you have landed your dream employees through a rigorous recruitment process, it is essential that you continue to invest in your decision by putting them through a thorough training process.

Training is actually an element of recruitment. A new employee's orientation and training sets the tone for their entire employment; this includes their impression of your business, its systems, and respect for its leaders. This has an impact on your ability to retain good people, and avoid unnecessary or redundant recruitment processes.

Too often, businesses rely on junior employees to train new ones without any guidelines or 'curriculum.' New employees are thrown into the deep end without clear expectations or an understanding of 'how things are done around here.'

These elements affect how an employee perceives their own required level of effort or performance. A business that doesn't give much thought to planning, expectations, and preparation will end up showing a new employee that the same lack of attention is expected from them.

Here are some things to ensure you implement when you create your comprehensive training system:

Prior Learning / Existing Knowledge

Acknowledge your new employee's prior learning, and don't overestimate or underestimate their existing knowledge.

Choice of Trainer

Make sure the person or people who will be training the new employee are sufficiently qualified and experienced. If an administrator is leading a salesperson's training and orientation, consider asking another salesperson or more senior team member to assist on specific days or sessions.

Training Materials

Have all the required training materials handy. This includes company manuals, industry guidebooks, common reference materials, work samples and anything else that will aid in the training efforts.

Training Tools

Also ensure you have the tools available to train your new recruit. Will the training be held at their workstation, or another workstation? Do you have all the software you need? All the equipment required? Doing so will ensure the training runs smoothly and the time provided will be used effectively.

Time

Provide more than ample time for training – including time for questions and elaboration. Rushing training benefits no one, including your profits.

Testing

Consider including some 'tests' or checks to ensure the new recruit understands each component of the training. Ask the trainer and the trainee to sign-off on each section.

The Big Picture

Each team member's role is part of a larger picture: the company as a whole. Ensure that the trainee understands how their role contributes to the big picture on each level. If they are a junior member of a department, they should understand how their job contributes to the department, as well as how the department contributes to the entire company.

Feedback

The trainee should be able to ask questions and review information at any time – including after the training process. Create an environment that encourages open dialogue and encourages employees to ask questions when they are unsure of a task.

The other common mistake that many companies make is ending training after the first few weeks of a new recruit's employment.

Training is an ongoing process for every single member of your team, and there should be a system or structure in place to ensure that staff training and development happens on a regular basis. This can include cross-training, employee development, and new systems orientation. Regular training not only benefits your staff and improves their performance, but it allows you – the business owner – to:

- Implement new policies + procedures
- Invest in your staff, thereby improving confidence and morale
- Evaluate staff performance at an individual and team level
- Reward staff based on performance improvements
- Provide a regular arena for feedback and discussion, including positive and negative experiences and issues

One-on-One Training + Evaluation

An effective system of ongoing training is weekly, monthly, or quarterly staff reviews. When conducted one-on-one, this provides a forum for regular communication with employees to review performance and identify areas for improvement. A one-on-one environment will encourage more open and honest dialogue than if the session were conducted as part of a team.

As a business owner, these sessions are valuable sources of information and insight into the strengths, weaknesses and motivations of your team.

If you have a large staff, consider pairing junior staff with senior staff and establishing mentorship relationships. This is a powerful way to build the synergy of your team, and frees you up from weekly meetings with each staff member. Instead, each senior staff member can report back to you on the results of their regular training sessions, and you only need to conduct these sessions with your senior staff.

Team Training

Team training events are great team builders, and provide insight into how your team interacts as a whole. These can take the form of "lunch and learns", where senior staff or guest speakers conduct an hour long session with staff members, or more social team building exercises with a less formal program.

Team training exercises will shed light on the leaders and followers in an organization and bring together employees who may work outside of the office. These can be especially helpful if you and your senior staff do not see the team 'in action' on a daily basis.

Keeping Your Dream Employees

Now that you have spent hours of time and potentially hundreds or thousands of dollars recruiting and training your staff, your human resource job is done, right?

I suppose you've done what you've set out to do: get the right people working for you. But what happens when those people get bored? Or stolen by another company? Or feel they've "done all they can do" at your company?

The final step in the overall recruitment process is employee retention. This includes keeping your employees happy, supporting their development, and giving them incentive to continuously improve their performance.

Environment

The environment you create for your staff has a huge impact on your employee retention rates. This includes the interior design and layout of your office or business, the lighting, plants, and kitchen amenities available. It also includes the culture of the company – what is the general working atmosphere? Are most people loud? Quiet? Is there a buzz or hum to the office space?

The bottom line is that employees should enjoy and feel comfortable coming to their workplace – they do spend most of their waking hours there.

Spending a little more on comfortable office furniture and amenities like coffee, tea, snacks and social spaces will go a long way toward keeping your employees happy at work.

Recognition, Rewards, and Incentive Programs

Did you know that many employees place more value on positive public recognition for a job well done than they do on salary?

Recognition and rewards are powerful tools when it comes to keeping employees happy. Positive feedback from those in more senior positions has a higher perceived value than a 3-5% salary increase – and it costs the business little to nothing to implement.

Incentive programs are a formalized way of rewarding employees for their achievements and successes. Clear targets and milestones are identified, and when an individual or team reaches those milestones they are rewarded with bonuses or prizes.

Recognition, rewards and incentive programs are an important part of employee retention, as well as team building. They will be discussed in further detail in the Team Building chapter.

Professional Development Programs

Another common reason employees choose to leave their positions is professional development. Many feel they need to move to another company in order to develop their careers or gain more responsibility. They may not necessarily dislike their current role, but become bored or stagnated and believe they have 'done all they can do' at that particular company.

Keeping good people means providing opportunities for growth and advancement within your company. This benefits the company because you can hire from within, and save money and time on recruiting and training new staff. It also benefits your employee and increases their loyalty toward your business.

Professional development programs are an important part of staff retention – but they are also an important part of business growth and development. A company with staff who are always increasing their knowledge and improving their skills will stay on the 'cutting edge' of their industry, and have an advantage over the competition.

Ongoing training and development should be a primary focus for any growing business. Here's why:

- Increases productivity
- Increases staff retention
- Increases workplace safety and morale
- Increases customer service
- Increases sales

Professional development programs typically focus on the big picture ambitions of the company and its staff members. The longer-term goals and career ambitions are recorded and taken into consideration.

Professional development can be easily worked into your ongoing one-on-one training systems. Keep a folder or binder for each staff member that outlines current role responsibilities, short and long term goals, and areas for improvement, and review it during your weekly or monthly meetings. Identify specific areas for growth, and develop plans of action for that growth.

For example, if your marketing assistant wants to grow into a marketing coordinator or manager role, and needs to improve her people management skills, consider putting her through a management course.

Maintaining this program doesn't have to be a time-consuming task. With some simple system tools and a commitment to regularly scheduled meetings, you can have a clear and effective program for your staff.

- Evolving job description document to monitor role responsibilities and tasks
- Regular performance evaluations
- Goal planning worksheets
- Continuing education programs at local business schools
- Regular meetings between staff and supervisors
- Rewards and incentives

8

Use Goal Setting Effectively

We've all heard about the power of setting goals. Everyone has surely seen statistics that connect goal setting to success in both your business life, and your personal life. I'm sure if I asked you today what your goals are, you could rattle off a few wants and hopes without thinking too long.

However, what most people do not realize is that the power of goal setting lies in *writing goals down*. Committing goals to paper and reviewing them regularly gives you a 95% higher chance of achieving your desired outcomes. Studies have shown that only three to five percent of people in the world have written goals – the same three to five percent who have achieve success in business and earn considerable wealth.

These studies have also found that by retirement, only four per cent of people in the world will have enough accumulated wealth to maintain their income level, and quality of life. As a business owner, it is essential that you develop a plan for your retirement, but it is equally essential that you develop a plan for your success.

This chapter focuses on the power of goal setting as part of your business success. We'll teach you to set SMART goals that are rooted in your own personal value system, and supporting techniques to achieve your goals faster.

What are Goals?

Goals are clear targets that are attached to a specific time frame and action plan; they focus your efforts, and drive your motivation in a clear direction. Goals are different from dreams in that they outline a plan of action, while dreams are a conceptual vision of your wish or desired outcome.

Goals require work; work on yourself, work for your business, and work for others. You cannot achieve a goal – no matter how badly you want it – without being prepared to make a considerable effort. If you are ready to invest your time and energy, goals will help you to:

- Realize a dream or wish for your personal or business life
- Make a change in your life – add positive, or remove negative
- Improve your skills and performance ability
- Start or change a habit – positive or negative

Why Set Goals?

As we've already reviewed, setting goals and committing them to paper is the most effective way to cultivate success. The most important reason to set a goal is **to attach a clear action plan to a desired outcome.**

Goals help focus our time and energy on one (or several) key outcome at a time. Many business owners have hundreds of ideas whirring around in their heads at any one time, on top of daily responsibilities. By writing down and focusing on a few ideas at a time, you can prioritize and concentrate your efforts, avoid being stretched too thin, and produce greater results.

Since goals attach action to outcomes, goals can help to break down big dreams into manageable (and achievable) sections. Creating a multi-goal strategy will put a road map in place to help you get to your desired outcome. If your goal is to start a pizza business and make six figures a year, there are a number of smaller steps to achieve before you achieve your end result.

Success doesn't happen by itself. It is the result of consistent and committed action by an individual who is driven to achieve something. Success means something different for everyone, so creating goals is a personal endeavor. Goals can be large and small, personal and public, financial and spiritual. It is not the size of the goal that matters; what matters is that you write the goal down and commit to making the effort required to achieve it.

What happens when I achieve a goal?

You should congratulate yourself and your team, of course! By rewarding yourself and your team after every achievement, you not only train your mind to associate hard work with reward, but develop loyalty among your employees.

You should also ask yourself if your achievement can be taken to the next level, or if your goal can be stretched by building on the effort you have already made. Consistently setting new and higher targets will lay the framework for constant improvement and personal and professional growth.

Power of Positive Thinking

When was the last time you tuned into your internal stream of consciousness? What does the stream of thoughts that run through your mind sound like? Are they positive? Negative? Are they logical? Reasonable?

Positive thinking and healthy self-talk are the most important business tools you can ever cultivate; by programming a positive stream of subconscious thoughts into your mind, you can control your reality, and ultimately your goals. Think about someone you know who is constantly negative; someone who complains and whines and makes excuses for their unhappiness. How successful are they? How do their fears and doubts become reality in their world?

You are what you continuously believe about yourself and your environment. If you focus your mind on something in your mental world, it will nearly always manifest as reality in your physical world.

Positive thinking is a key part of setting goals. You won't achieve your goal until you believe that you can. You will achieve your goals faster when you believe in yourself, and the people around you who are helping to make your goal a reality.

Successful people are rooted in a strong belief system – belief in themselves, belief in the work they are doing, and belief in the people around them. They are motivated to improve and learn, but also confident in their existing skills and knowledge. Their positive attitude and energy is clearly felt in everything they do.

Ever notice how complainers usually surround themselves with other complainers? The same is true of positive thinkers. If you cultivate an upbeat and positive attitude, you will be surrounded by people who share your values and outlook on life.

Too often, people and our society subscribe to a continuous stream of negative chatter. The more you hear it, the more you'll believe it.

How many times have you heard:

- That's impossible.
- Don't even bother.
- It's already been done.
- We tried that, and it didn't work.
- You're too young.
- You're too old.
- You'll never get there.
- You'll never get that done.
- You can't do that.

Positive thinking and positive influences will provide the support you need to achieve your goals. Choose your friends and close colleagues wisely, and surround yourself with positive thinkers.

Creating SMART Goals

SMART goals are just that: smart. Whether you are setting goals for your personal life, your business, or with your employees, goals that have been developed with the SMART principle have a higher probability of being achieved.

The SMART Principle

1. Specific

Specific goals are clearer and easier to achieve than nonspecific goals. When writing down your goal, ask yourself the five "W" questions to narrow in on what exactly you are aiming for. Who? Where? What? When? Why?

For example, instead of a nonspecific goal like, "get in shape for the summer," a specific goal would be, "go to the gym three times a week and eat twice as many vegetables."

2. Measurable

If you can't measure your goal, how will you know when you've achieved it? Measurable goals help you clearly see where you are, and where you want to be. You can see change happen as it happens.

Measurable goals can also be broken down and managed in smaller pieces. They make it easier to create an action plan or identify the steps required to achieve your goal. You can track your progress, revise your plan, and celebrate each small achievement. For example, instead of aiming to increase revenue in 2009, you can set out to increase revenue by 30% in the next 12 months, and celebrate each 10% along the way.

3. Achievable

Goals that are achievable have a higher chance of being realized. While it is important to think big, and dream big, too often people set goals that are simply beyond their capabilities and wind up disappointed. Goals can stretch you, but they should always be feasible to maintain your motivation and commitment.

For example, if you want to complete your first triathlon but you've never run a mile in your life, you would be setting a goal that was beyond your current capabilities. If you decided instead to train for a five mile race in six months, you would be setting an achievable goal.

4. Relevant

Relevant – or realistic – goals are goals that have a logical place in your life or your overall business strategy. The goal's action plan can be reasonably integrated into your life, with a realistic amount of effort.

For example, if your goal is to train to climb to base camp at Mount Everest within one year and you're about to launch a start-up business, you may need to question the relevance of your goal in the context of your current commitments.

5. Timely

It is essential for every goal to be attached to a time-frame – otherwise it is merely a dream. Check in to make sure that your time-frame is realistic - not too short, or too long. This will keep you motivated and committed to your action plan, and allow you track your progress.

Autosuggestion + Visualization

Autosuggestion and visualization are two techniques that can assist you in achieving your goals. Some of the most well-known and successful people in the world use these techniques, and it is not coincidence that they are masters in their own fields of business and sport. A few of these people include:

- Michael Phelps (Olympic Swimmer)
- Andre Agassi (Tennis)
- Donald Trump (Real Estate)
- Wayne Gretzky (Hockey)
- Bill Gates (Microsoft)
- Walt Disney (Entertainment)

Of course, each of these people have a high degree of talent, ambition, intelligence and drive. However, to reach the top of their respective field, they have each used Autosuggestion and Visualization.

Autosuggestion

Autosuggestion is your internal dialogue; the constant stream of thoughts and comments that flows through your mind, and impacts what you think about yourself and how you perceive situations.

Since you were a small child, this self-talk has been influenced by your experiences and has programmed your mind to think and react in certain ways. The good news is that you can reprogram your mind and customize your self-talk any way you like. That is the power of Autosuggestion.

To begin practicing Autosuggestion, make sure you are relaxed and open to trying the technique; an ideal time is just before bed, or when you have some time to sit quietly. Then, repeat positive affirmations to yourself about the ideal outcome. Top sports and business people will often practice just before a big game or meeting.

Some examples of positive self-talk or autosuggestion include:

- I will lead my team to a victory tonight!
- I will be relaxed open to meeting new people at the party tonight!
- I will deliver a clear and impacting speech!
- I will stop worrying and tackle this problem tomorrow!
- I will stand up for my own ideas in the meeting!
- I will remember everything I have studied for the test tomorrow!

Visualization

Visualization is a practice complementary to Autosuggestion. While you can repeat affirmations to yourself over and over, combining this practice with visualization is twice as powerful.

Visualization is exactly what it sounds like: repeatedly visualizing how something is going to happen in your mind's eye. Nearly everyone in sports practices this technique. It has been proven to enhance performance better than practice alone.

This technique can easily be applied to business. For example, prior to any presentation or meeting where you must speak, present or "perform." You can also visualize yourself being incredibly productive and effective in your office. Or, having a discussion with your spouse calmly and rationally.

Elements to think about during visualization:

- What does the room look like?
- What do the people in the room look like?
- What is their mood? How do they receive me?
- What image do I project?
- How do I look?
- How do I behave? What is my attitude?
- What is the outcome?

9

Creating Effective
Marketing Material

Your marketing collateral gets sent out in the world to do one thing: act as an ambassador for your product or service, in place of *you*. This may seem like a big job for a piece of paper, but it's a helpful way to think about the materials you create.

When you meet with a potential or existing client, you do a number of things. You make sure you are well prepared with all the information the customer could need. You dress in clothing that is appropriate. You anticipate their needs, and offer a solution to their problems. You may also cater to how they best like to receive information.

Chances are, you wouldn't meet with clients just for the sake of meeting with a client – say, for instance, to show off your new suit. Likewise, you shouldn't create and distribute collateral that is non-essential.

We all know that the biggest challenge for small businesses is the limited number of zeros attached to their marketing budget. Marketing materials can be expensive, and a single, well-produced piece has the ability to devour the entire budget. Given that billion-dollar marketing campaigns fail every day, how can you be sure to make the most of, and be successful with, the dollars you're working within?

The answer? Limit yourself to only the essential items for your individual business, and produce them *well* with the resources you have.

Your Essential Marketing Materials

The easiest way to throw away your marketing budget is to create and produce marketing materials *you don't need*. Since many pieces of collateral are paper-based, this not only leaves you with boxes of extra (outdated) materials, but also takes a huge toll on the environment.

Take some time to determine what marketing materials you do need, and stick to your list. It's easy to want to "keep up with the Joneses" when your competition comes out with a new piece, but remember your focus should be on attracting and retaining a customer base, not matching the competition item for item.

Know your target market. Make sure you have a solid understanding of your customer base. From that knowledge, you can easily determine what the best way is to reach out and communicate with them. Are they a paper-based or techno savvy client group? Do they appreciate being contacted by email or mail? Are they impressed by flashy design, or simple pieces? *How* you communicate is often just as or more important than *what* you communicate.

Pay attention to costs. Do you really need a die-cut business card? Does your flyer absolutely require ink to the edges? Unique touches to marketing collateral can grab a customer's attention, but they can also dramatically increase the cost of production. Keep an eye out during the design process and make strategic choices about graphic elements.

Make mistakes – in small batches. Not sure if that flyer is going to do the trick? Testing out a limited time offer? Small production runs may cost a little more, but you'll avoid collecting boxes of unusable materials. Or, try a split run with type versions of the same piece and see what works best.

Keep the environment in mind. Environmental responsibility is on everyone's mind these days – including your customers. Always question if a particular marketing item can be produced in electronic format. Consider eliminating plastic bags in exchange for cloth ones, printed with your logo; print everything double-sided; send electronic newsletters; use your website to communicate; and, use recycled paper and envelopes when you can.

Brainstorm your wish list. Create a list of desired marketing materials, and ignore expenses, clients, or any other constraint. Then, beside each item, indicate realistically if it is a needed, wanted, not needed, or electronic item. The next page includes a checklist to get you started. Once you have finished, re-write your list in priority order. This will keep you focused on the essentials only.

Marketing Materials Checklist

Item	Need	Want	Don't Need	Electronic
Logo				
Business Cards				
Brochure				
Website				
Newsletter				
Catalogue				
Advertisements				
Flyers				
Fridge Magnet				
Branded Swag (pens, etc.)				
Employee Clothing				
Product Labels				
Signage				
Internal Templates (Fax Cover, Memo, etc.)				
Email Signature				
Blog				
Letterhead + Envelopes				
Thank You Cards				
Notepads				
Seasonal Gifts				
Company Profile				

Headlines + Sub headlines

If your headlines were all a potential customer read, how do you think your marketing materials would fare? Headlines need to be bold, dramatic, shocking and absolutely answer the questions "What's in it for me?" or, "Why should I care?"

Headlines (and sub headlines) are vital in today's market because we are bombarded with so much information that we scan everything. Readers are skimming your materials to find out why they should bother paying attention to your product or service. Hit their hot buttons, and tell them why they should care, in your headlines!

Remember that headlines and sub headlines are not just for advertisements. They work wonders in newsletters, sales letters, brochures and websites, and can be incorporated into all of your essential marketing materials.

Design

The cost of professional design can eat up the majority of your marketing budget in a hurry. However, the cost of distributing materials that look and feel unprofessional can often be much higher. The key is to find the middle ground.

Unless you have design or desktop publishing experience – or even if you do – your time is probably not best spent designing your own marketing materials. Depending on the size of your business and your graphic needs (i.e., Do you need frequent photography of your products?) there are a number of options you can choose from:

1. **Hire a design agency.** This is no doubt the most costly of your options. However, if you have a number of items to be designed, you may be able to get a package rate. Another option is to have the design agency create a logo and stationery package for you, then create a "how-to" guide for use of the logo, fonts, and other graphic elements in the rest of your marketing materials.

2. **Hire a freelance designer.** For most small businesses, the benefits of using a freelance designer (aside from cost savings) are convenience and trust. If you are lucky enough to find one you work well with, work hard to establish a seamless working relationship and you'll never worry about the design of your marketing materials again. Ask colleagues for recommendations of local designers, or post an ad on craigslist.

3. **Hire a part-time design employee.** Need to hire someone part-time for a task around the office or shop? Consider recruiting someone with design skills and hiring them for full-time work. This could include graphic design students, or someone with an interest (and talent) in the field.

Whichever option you choose – or if you choose to design your materials yourself - the two most important things to remember about design are:

1. **Keep it consistent.** Your marketing materials must be consistent, or your customers will never learn to recognize your brand.

2. **Keep it simple.** Simple, clean design is the most effective way of communicating. Use "wow" pieces sparingly.

Guidelines for the Top 10 Marketing Materials

Logo

- **Use design resources.** If you are going to spend any money on outside design help, this is the time to do it. Your logo is the visual representation of your product or service, and appears on everything that relates to your business. This is the core of your brand image, and needs to be done right the first time.

- **Remember the purpose.** The logo needs to be a unique reflection of your business, your business values, and the industry you work in. Before you commit to your logo, make sure to give careful consideration to color choice, image selection and image recognition – as well as the logos that already exist in the marketplace. Test it out on your family and friends for an outside opinion and use their feedback.

- **Don't get too complicated.** Can it be produced (and seen clearly) in black and white? In a single color? With your company name? Too often businesses design their own logos that include a complex assortment of photos, words, and solid design elements. These do not photocopy well, and can't be clearly read at a small scale. Keep your logo design down to a graphic image and the name of your business.

Business cards

- **Cover the basics**. A business card needs to communicate your basic contact information to potential clients, including who you are and *what your business does*. Make sure you've covered the basics and made it easy for them to be in touch.

  - Name
  - Title
  - Company Name
  - Company Slogan / Description
  - Phone Number

  - Email Address
  - Fax Number
  - Address
  - Cell Number (if applicable)
  - Website

- **Make it memorable. Be creative.** Choose interesting shapes, die-cuts, orientation (vertical vs. horizontal), bright colors, and unique materials (wood, plastic, magnet, aluminum or foam). You don't have to go crazy or spend lots of money to do this – simple, clever twists on basic design make an impact. Just keep it relevant to your product or service.

- **Give them a reason to keep it.** What is going to keep them from throwing it out, or filing it in a 3" binder of other cards? Make the card worth keeping by adding something useful to the backside. For example, coffee shops put frequent buyer incentives on the backside of their cards, encouraging customers to keep them in their wallets. Other examples include pick-up schedules, reminders, calendars, testimonials, or coupons.

- **Produce a high quality card.** Use at least 100lb card stock, and print in color. Choose clear, easy to read fonts that aren't any smaller than 9pt.

Letterhead

- **Ensure a professional quality.** Letterhead that is simple, clean, and well produced allows the reader to focus on the important part: the content. Have your letterhead professionally printed on 32lb paper, or choose a textured stock. Show that you are invested in the professionalism of your company.

- **Pay attention to design choices.** The design of your marketing collateral should reflect your corporate values and the personality of your organization. If you are environmentally conscious, choose recycled paper and write it in small print at the bottom of the page. Letterhead can also be a place for subtle graphic elements, like watermarks, in addition to your logo.

- **Keep consistent with other materials.** Your letterhead is part of your stationery package, and should look and feel the same as the rest of your pieces. For example, if your business cards have been printed with rounded corners, so should your letterhead. Use consistent fonts, colors, and logo placement on your letterhead, business cards, fax cover sheets, and other internal documents to ensure recognition and ease of readability.

Brochures

- **Cover the basics.** Each brochure you produce should include your basic marketing message, USP, and detailed company contact information. Product or service features, and customer benefits should be clearly displayed and described.

- **Be purpose-focused.** Why are you producing this brochure? Are you featuring a new product line? Trying to increase awareness? Introducing your service to a new market? Stay closely connected to the purpose behind your brochure, and ensure that all of the information (and images) in the brochure support that purpose.

- **Keep it simple.** Make sure the design and information organization is clean and easy to navigate. Like advertisements, leaving blank spaces gives the reader a break and makes it easier to narrow in on key messages.

- **Choose high quality production.** If you don't invest in your business, why should anyone else? Produce your brochure on high quality paper, in vivid color, and have it professionally folded. An impressive-looking brochure will travel farther than a homemade one – from one client's hands to another's.

- **Keep it fresh.** If you produce brochures on a regular basis, consider giving each a theme to distinguish the information as new and interesting. Keep the overall look and feel consistent, but play with images and content layout to revitalize the design.

Newsletters

- **Be in touch.** Don't wait until your existing clients walk back into your store. Show them they're important to your business, and keep them updated on new products and services by keeping distributing a personalized newsletter.

- **Use an online distribution service.** Online email marketing tools (CRM tools) have never been easier or cheaper to use, and enable you to personalize your letters without much effort. They will also track for you which clients open their newsletters, and which click through to your website.

- **Provide information, tell a story.** Engage the reader with a short anecdote, or a piece of relevant information. Many people are bombarded by hard-copy and electronic letters on a daily basis, so make sure yours is worthy of their reading time. Include an "experts corner" or "new product feature" and structure the newsletter like your own business newspaper. Add links to relevant media articles, or special offers.

- **Choose a frequency you can maintain.** Newsletters can be time consuming, so be realistic about how often you promise to distribute them. This depends on your resources, and the needs of your business, but generally once a month to once every three months is a good time frame.

Company (or Corporate) Profile

- **Your ultimate company brochure.** Your company profile includes all pertinent information on your business and your offering, and acts as the base for all other marketing items. These are generally longer pieces – from five to 20 pages in length, allowing you ample room for written and visual content.

- **Tell your story.** The company profile is the place to tell the story of your business. Engage the reader, use anecdotes, and describe how and why your company was created. If you inherited the family business, describe how you're carrying on tradition and instilling new life. If you created your company from scratch with your college roommate, let the reader know. These real life details are interesting and establish trust with your potential clients and associates.

- **Communicate your values.** Here you have the space to describe your company's vision, values and approach, or philosophies. Make sure you relate your values to your offering, and keep this section short and succinct.

- **Explain your offering – features, benefits and all.** Just like your brochure, make sure to describe the full features and benefits of your product or service. Sprinkle testimonials throughout the design to back up your statements. This can include your full range of services, or simply an overview of your product types. Use professional images and creative copy to keep readers engaged.

- **Choose high-quality design and production.** Spend time creating a company profile that will last. Then, spend money producing one that will impress. Choose glossy paper, and a high-quality press, and leave the profiles around your store and office for clients to read and admire.

Signage

- **Get professional advice.** Outdoor signage can be a daunting task for anyone who hasn't designed, produced, or otherwise gone through the process. Since signage is influenced by a variety of factors – one of which is your municipal government signage bylaw – you may wish to enlist the help of a professional (a signage designer or printer) to guide you through the process and avoid costly errors.

- **Make it visible.** All of your outdoor signage should be easily seen from the street, or within the plaza or complex you are located in. In some cases, you may need more than one sign to do this. Keep in mind how your sign will look at night, as well as during the day, as your company logo and phone number or website needs to be visible at all times.

- **Make it distinct.** When it comes to signage, you can get really creative with materials, lights, and colors. While you need to maintain logo, color, and font consistency, you can add other graphic elements that may not work on the rest of your collateral, including 3D elements and window treatments. Make it memorable.

- **Remember your indoor signage.** Every business needs indoor signage to continually remind customers where they are. This includes section signage, product signage, way finding systems, and promotion announcements. If your business is located in an office, consider signage with your logo and company name above the reception area. Again, keep this signage consistent with the rest of your company materials, and you will be contributing to brand recognition.

Advertisements + Flyers

- **Place ads strategically.** Once you have determined who your target market is, you need to focus on advertising in the publications they are most likely to read, and distributing flyers in places they are most likely to be. Spend ad dollars strategically, and don't spend them all at once. Take time to test what publications work, and which don't by measuring the response from each placement. And, when you place ads, request placement that is well-forward and in the top right hand corner.

- **Grab their attention.** You have less than half a second to grab the attention of your audience with print advertising, so use it wisely. Spend the bulk of your time crafting the headline and choosing compelling images.

- **Keep their attention.** If you caught their attention, you have another two seconds to keep it. Use subheadings to further entice them to read on for the details of your product or service offer.

- **Tell them why they should buy.** Always include your marketing message or USP in your advertising. Describe the features and benefits of your product or service, but focus on the benefits that will trigger an emotional response from your target audience – love, money, luxury, convenience, and security.

- **Tell them how they can buy.** Include a call to action beside your contact information, and include your phone number, website address, and business address (if applicable). You may wish to include a scarcity or urgency offer to compel your readers to act fast.

- **Know the importance of white space.** If you try to cram too much information into your ad or flyer, your readers will skip it. Clean, clear, easy to read ads and one-page flyers with succinct messages are most effective.

Website

- **Be purpose-focused.** Like your brochure, your website can serve a number of purposes. To be effective, you need to narrow in on the specific purpose when designing the content structure of the pages. Who is your audience? What do you want them to leave the site knowing? What do you want the site to make them do? Visit your store? Buy your offering? Pick up the phone? Make sure you are clear on this point before you start.

- **Make the address easy to remember (and find!).** A website address that is too long or too complicated will not get remembered, or found. Do a search for available website addresses that relate to your business or marketing message, and try to secure a site with a

.com ending. If your company name is taken, use your USP or guarantee instead.

- **Focus on content.** The overall structure of how you organize the content on your site is like the foundation of your house. You can change the paint color, and the furniture, but the foundation is more or less there for good. Before you work with a designer and create the visual fabric of your website, focus on creating solid copy that is clearly organized. Put together a map of your structure, starting with your homepage and subpages, and allocating specific content to each page.

- **Revitalize regularly.** Your company is always changing, and so should your website. This is an important (and relatively inexpensive) way to communicate your company news and achievements, and most likely the easiest accessed source of information. Have areas for easy content updates – like a "news" section – and make sure sections like "employees" and "services" are kept up to date. For larger updates, go back to your purpose and website map, and make sure the content changes still support the original intent of the website.

- **Organize for intuition.** Make key information easy to access – especially your contact information. You can quickly tell if a website is easy to navigate, because the information you are looking for appears in a natural order. For example, when visiting a restaurant website, a link to the reservations page is provided on the menu page. While you're putting together your website map, do some research online and investigate what does and doesn't work. A good rule of thumb is to ensure it takes no more than three clicks to access a page. Bury content too deep, and your audience will get frustrated and leave.

- **Keep consistent with marketing materials.** Your website is an extension of your marketing campaign, and should be treated as such. Use consistent logo placements, fonts, colors and images so that all elements of your collateral are unified. Likewise with marketing campaigns. If you are running a new promotion, or featuring a new item in an advertisement, include that information on your website. Customers responding to the ad will be reinforced, and customers who did not see the ad will be aware of the offer.

- **Measure your results.** Your website is a piece of your marketing collateral, just like brochures and advertisements, and should be evaluated for effectiveness on a regular basis. Easy website analysis tools, like Google Analytics, will show you which pages your audience is viewing, how long they're staying on each page, and where and when they leave the site. That is powerful information when it comes to structuring content, and choosing which page to put your most important messages.

10

How to Use Testimonials and Profit from Social Proof

The Power of Testimonials

Testimonials are simply the single most powerful asset you can have in your marketing toolkit. When your customers tell others about the benefits of choosing your business, it is a thousand times more powerful than the same words from your mouth.

The words and opinions of others motivate people to spend money every day. From celebrity endorsements on TV and in magazines, to casual conversations with friends, decisions about what product or service to buy – and what brand or provider – are heavily influenced by those who have purchased before.

Why? There are several reasons. Many people have an inherent distrust of salespeople, and a skepticism toward marketing materials. Others are bombarded with choice, and are looking for some sense of security in their purchase decision.

Testimonials build the credibility of your business, break down natural barriers, and create a sense of trust for the consumer. They have an incredible ability to persuade customers to buy, and to buy from you. Think about the last time someone recommended a brand of laundry detergent, a bottle of wine, or a plumber to you. Their positive experience had more of an impact on your decision to buy than any advertisement or discount.

When it comes to spending money, people want a sure bet. They want to know that someone else has bought before, and they want to know that the product or service has delivered the promised results. A testimonial for your business is worth more than any copywriter, clever ad slogan, or sales pitch.

Customers Who Give Testimonials

When people put their name and reputation on paper to endorse something, it creates a sense of loyalty; if questioned, they will back their decision, even if they find later their decision was wrong.

When someone is willing to endorse your product or service in writing, they have likely already started a word-of-mouth chain of verbal testimonials about their positive experience. Remember the last time you discovered a chiropractic miracle worker? Or the fastest and cheapest drycleaner? Didn't you tell every one of your friends who could use the service?

By asking a customer for a testimonial, you are asking for their assistance in the growth of your business. When they feel they are truly helping and participating in the development of your company, their sense of pride will mean continuous loyalty to your product or service.

11 Ways to Get Great Testimonials

Testimonials are powerful – no question. But how do you make sure that the quotes you get from your customers will bring you the most value? How do you ensure that your client will articulate your product's merits in a clear and easy to understand way? How do you make sure you can actually use their testimonials in your marketing materials?

Asking for testimonials requires more effort than merely soliciting general comments and praise. You want to ensure that your customer feels a sense of pride and loyalty in providing their opinion, and that their opinion will have an impact on potential buyers.

How? Glad you asked. Here are 11 proven ways to get great testimonials from your customers.

1. Don't wait!

Your customers are the happiest and most willing to help you within a day to a week of their purchase, so aim to secure the testimonial in this time period. Ask for the testimonial before they leave, and make sure you have all their contact details to follow up with. This also ensures you stay on top of your testimonial recruitment!

2. Get specific

Specific testimonials are more believable. The more specific you can have your customer be, the stronger and more impactful the testimonial will be. Remember the Sleep Country testimonials that referenced the little "booties" that their delivery men wore to keep carpets clean? Meaningful details get remembered. Ask for mention of things like time, dates, extraordinary customer service, and personal observations.

3. If you were the solution – what was the problem?

Testimonials that tell stories are more engaging. Ask client to not only describe their experience with your company, but also the negative experience that led them to your door. If they can describe the struggles and challenges they were facing before receiving your service, the reader will likely be able to sympathize and resonate with similar struggles. This will motivate them to solve their problems with your solution.

4. Write the first draft

Make it easy for your clients. This technique is something you can offer someone who is hesitant to commit to writing a testimonial due to time constraints, or is procrastinating. Ask them to brainstorm a few notes they would like to include in their feedback, write them down, and string them into a concise testimonial for their review. All they have to do is review, print on their letterhead, sign, and mail back to you!

5. Include your marketing message or USP

Always ask your customers to include your unique selling proposition (USP) in the testimonial. For instance, if your USP includes exceptional customer service, same-day installation, and a money-back guarantee then ask your customer to attest to those qualities.

6. A picture says...

Yes, you know the saying. But it's true. When readers attach an image of the speaker to words, the words are enlivened and have twice as much validity and impact. When readers see an image of a previous client using your product or service, their words and opinions are even more believable. You can take these simple pictures yourself – and take many so you have a selection to choose from.

7. Credentials equal trust

As we mentioned, testimonials from credible sources will have the most believability and impact. When you ask for a testimonial, make sure your customer states their expertise and credentials. If you sell custom orthotics, and can secure a solid testimonial from a doctor, their words will be golden in your marketing materials.

8. Don't forget to ask permission

When you ask for testimonials, make sure you are clear that their words may be used in your marketing materials, including advertisements, website and in-store displays. This is a good time to thank them for their time and sincerity, and show your appreciation for their words.

9. Location, location...

Depending on the market reach of your business, the location of your customers is an important part of the believability of your testimonial. If you own a community-based business, when potential clients see you've made others happy just down their street they'll be motivated to use your service too. If you own a regional business, then the cities and addresses of other happy customers can help communicate the reach of your service.

10. Testimonials are not surveys

Keep the purpose of your request in mind when you're asking for testimonials. Testimonials should be positive fodder for your advertising materials. Surveys are used to solicit meaningful (and often confidential) customer information to refine and improve your service. Testimonials are public statements, while surveys are often anonymous and can produce less-than-positive results.

11. Say thank you!

Thanking a customer for their time and effort creating your testimonial is just plain good manners. It also increases loyalty and goodwill. This can be done via email, but sending a formal letter on your letterhead is a more meaningful approach.

Using Testimonials Strategically

So now you have a pile of glowing customer testimonials. What's next?

Choose the most powerful piece of the testimonial

What is the most convincing aspect of the testimonial? Is it the author? Where they are from? A specific sentence or paragraph they wrote? Be strategic about the aspect of the testimonial that you feature, and select what will have the most impact.

For example, you can compile a list titled *What Customers are Saying*, and list only the phrases that support your specific marketing message. Or you can feature the unique credentials or story of your customer, before you even include their testimonial. You can also summarize the testimonial with a powerful headline.

Put them on your website

Adding a page of testimonials to your website is a great start, especially when you're beginning to solicit customer responses. However, the most powerful way to ensure site visitors actually see your testimonials is to include them on every page – especially the ones with the highest traffic.

A testimonial should be placed wherever you make a strong statement about your service or product, and wherever the service or product is described. This is a great way to break up your sales copy with some "proof". As they read about your offering, your credibility will be validated by someone other than you.

Compile your best 25 to 50 letters in a display book

Like a proud grandparent, keep a book of testimonials in the waiting area of your office, your boardroom, and in your desk. Or, put one at the service counter, cash register and anywhere else people may have a moment to flip through.

I've seen this done in recruiting firm, a hardware store, and a physiotherapist's office. When clients have a chance to read the positive experiences of others, they will be more open to hearing your sales pitch less guarded when responding to your unique offering.

Hang your favorite testimonials in your store or office

Testimonials as art! Frame your favorite testimonials – preferably the ones written on client letterhead – and post them on the wall in your business. Even if clients don't read them up close, the volume and visual recognition of client logos will have impact. Plus – your next satisfied clients will want to see their company names on the wall too.

Put them in your advertisements

Use short, clear, concise testimonials in your advertising. When was the last time you saw a prescription drug advertisement without a testimonial? Can't remember? That's because you haven't. The best advertisers know that testimonials are the fastest and most effective way to overcome skepticism and get clients thinking that your product or service is the solution to their problem.

Include a page of testimonials in your direct mail

When sending your marketing materials directly to a mass list of potential clients, let the words of others speak to the merits of your product or service. Put together a page or two of testimonials, and attach it to your mailing. The credibility of your company will be instantly established, encouraging clients to act – and buy – faster.

Partner with an associate for joint mailing

If you have an associate or colleague who has a similar customer base of new prospects for your business, try a joint-endorsed mailing. Each of you will send a letter to your own clients, endorsing the other's products and services. Your service or solution is offered to a potential client by a trusted source, and you are offering your existing clients the added value of an associate's service to complement your own.

Testimonial Request Letter

Here is an example of a basic testimonial request letter that can be customized and made into a template for your unique business. This can also be sent over email if that is how your clients prefer to be contacted.

Mr. John Smith
1234 Main Street

Anytown, Anyplace 90210

January 2, 2006

Dear Mr. Smith,

Thank you for visiting our store this week. It was a pleasure helping you select a new laptop for your daughter to use at university this fall – they just grow up too fast! Your research and clear idea of the product you were searching for truly made our job easy. We love the back to school season, because it means working with clients like yourself.

We know there are a lot of choices when it comes to purchasing a laptop in Anytown, so thank you for choosing ABC Company. If there is anything else we can assist you with, please don't hesitate to contact me directly.

We occasionally ask select customers for their feedback in the form of a testimonial. Because we are so proud of the feedback we receive, we often use our customer's quotes in our marketing materials – specifically our website and sales brochures. The real life experiences of our customers at ABC Company are stories that we are proud of.

Could I ask you to write down some of your feedback? A few words about your experience with ABC Company, and how we helped you and your daughter would be greatly appreciated. We encourage you to print this on your company letterhead, so we can provide your own company with some exposure as well.

You may want to include the names of the associates who helped you, and how your daughter is enjoying her laptop. Again, we would like to feature your name and experience in our marketing materials. For your convenience, I've included a prepaid envelope with which to mail your testimonial back to us.

Thank you very much for your assistance.

Kind regards,

Your name here

Testimonial Thank You Letter

Here is an example of a short thank you letter for a testimonial that can also be customized and made into a template for your unique business. You may wish to write your thank you letters on company note cards, but try to avoid sending these thank you's via email.

Mr. John Smith
1234 Main Street
Anytown, Anyplace 90210

January 10, 2006

Dear Mr. Smith,

We received your glowing testimonial in the mail today, and I wanted to thank you personally for your kind words. Your comments about our store and our people are important to us, and I will make sure my staff takes a moment to read your letter.

We are thrilled that your daughter is enjoying her laptop, and using it to keep in touch with you while she studies abroad. When we sold it to you, we truly believed it would provide the most long-lasting value for her student budget. I hope it serves her for the rest of her time at school.

Thank you again for taking the time to write us. We are all proud to have been of service to you and your daughter, and look forward to seeing you both again soon.

Warm regards,

Your Name Here

Testimonial Examples

Below you will find a series of sample testimonials, and excerpts from testimonial letters. Read these over, and take a moment to notice why each is a powerful statement. We have also summarized each testimonial with a headline.

24% Response Rate from a Single Direct Mailing!

We were skeptical about direct mail campaigns, and unsure about the return on investment. Your strategic advice and logistical help made the project run smoothly and easily – we received over 200 leads from this single effort!

John and Betty McFee
Scottsdale, AZ

Best Sleep in 20 Years!

I can't tell you how much I appreciated Craig's patience and assistance in my mattress selection. He is so knowledgeable of each mattress' design and features, and helped us find a financing solution that worked with our budget. I haven't slept this well in over two decades. Promote him!

Jason Carmichael

Gentle and effective approach

I have always been reluctant to visit a chiropractor for my lower back pain because I am not comfortable with physical adjustments. Sarah took the time to clearly explain the cause of my pain, and gave me easy exercises to help correct the problem. She respected my comfort level, and treated me without uncomfortable cracks and snaps!

Wally Orton

Testimonial Worksheet

Start today! Brainstorm a list of recent customers and clients who you will approach for testimonials. Post this worksheet in your office, and track your progress. Aim for 50 testimonials in two months. You can never have too many.

Name + Phone	Request Letter Sent	Follow Up Call Made	Testimonial Received	Thank-you Letter Sent
	☐	☐	☐	☐
	☐	☐	☐	☐
	☐	☐	☐	☐
	☐	☐	☐	☐
	☐	☐	☐	☐
	☐	☐	☐	☐
	☐	☐	☐	☐
	☐	☐	☐	☐
	☐	☐	☐	☐
	☐	☐	☐	☐
	☐	☐	☐	☐
	☐	☐	☐	☐
	☐	☐	☐	☐
	☐	☐	☐	☐
	☐	☐	☐	☐
	☐	☐	☐	☐
	☐	☐	☐	☐
	☐	☐	☐	☐

So What Do You Do From Here?

Take Action! If you're already an accomplished business owner and earning in excess of $250,000.00 per year (rich according to the Federal Government), use this book as direction to enhance the speed of your business success. If you are not as accomplished as you would like to be then the smartest thing to do is...

A) Adopt a Growth Mindset

B) Model Success

C) Find Someone to Hold You Accountable

Concentrate on strategies to LEARN and the EARN will follow! If you are serious about taking the next step then go to work on yourself, study other business successes, understand marketing strategies and become a sponge for new (proven) material. The amazing thing about the game of business is that when you put proven processes to work and continue to follow them, an abundance of success will follow. The biggest mistake is to start a process and then fallback into your old habits after a short time.

Above all, get the knowledge you need before you step onto the field. Think about it... if you were going to challenge Michael Jordan to a game of H O R S E for money, wouldn't it make sense to learn the game and practice before you stepped on the court to play him? It is amazing to me how many new small business people start the game of business against seasoned professionals (the competition), without first developing the necessary knowledge to be successful. Then they fail and blame the market, the economy, their location, etc.

If you have a business and have not yet managed to start to create wealth and systems that allow you to take time off, build retirement accounts or pay for your children's college, then learn and master the steps outlined in my book. I am a huge advocate of education and mentors. Get the right information, find someone that knows how to walk you through them and watch your quality of life take new shape.

To learn how to avoid the 3 key mistakes all small business owners make, visit www.RobertTuckerUniversity.com